CHINESE NAMES, SURNA[MES]

LOCATIONS & ADDRESSES

中国大陆地址集

GUANGXI ZHUANG AUTONOMOUS REGION - PART 7

广西壮族自治区

ZIYUE TANG

汤子玥

ACKNOWLEDGEMENT

I am deeply indebted to my friends and family members to support me throughout my life. Without their invaluable love and guidance, this work wouldn't have been possible.

Thank you

Ziyue Tang

汤子玥

PREFACE

The book introduces foreigner students to the Chinese names along with locations and addresses from the **Guangxi Zhuang Autonomous Region** of China (中国广西壮族自治区). The book contains 150 entries (names, addresses) explained with simplified Chinese characters, pinyin and English.

Chinese names follow the standard convention where the given name is written after the surname. For example, in 王威 (Wang Wei), Wang is the surname, and Wei is the given name. Further, the surnames are generally made of one (王) or two characters (司马). Similarly, the given names are also made of either one or two characters. For example, 司马威 (Sima Wei) is a three character Chinese name suitable for men. 司马威威 is a four character Chinese name.

Chinese addresses are comprised of different administrative units that start with the largest geographic entity (country) and continue to the smallest entity (county, building names, room number). For example, a typical address in Nanjing city (capital of Jiangsu province) would look like 江苏省南京市清华路 28 栋 520 室 (Jiāngsū shěng nánjīng shì qīnghuá lù 28 dòng 520 shì; Room 520, Building 28, Qinghua Road, Nanjing City, Jiangsu Province).

CONTENTS

CHAPTER 1: NAME, SURNAME & ADDRESSES (1-30)

900。姓名: 逢化冠

住址（寺庙）：广西壮族自治区河池市都安瑶族自治县科桥路 962 号智乐寺（邮政编码：824104）。联系电话：60129920。电子邮箱：qljnb@onysgrxl.god.cn

Zhù zhǐ: Páng Huā Guān Guǎngxī Zhuàngzú Zìzhìqū Héchí Shì Dū Ān Yáozú Zìzhìxiàn Kē Qiáo Lù 962 Hào Zhì Lè Sì (Yóuzhèng Biānmǎ：824104). Liánxì Diànhuà：60129920. Diànzǐ Yóuxiāng：qljnb@onysgrxl.god.cn

Hua Guan Pang, Zhi Le Temple, 962 Ke Qiao Road, Duan Yao Autonomous County, Hechi, Guangxi Autonomous Region. Postal Code: 824104. Phone Number：60129920. E-mail：qljnb@onysgrxl.god.cn

901。姓名: 池计鸣

住址（家庭）：广西壮族自治区南宁市马山县铁寰路 425 号食冠公寓 5 层 955 室（邮政编码：568160）。联系电话：40421249。电子邮箱：qovme@aicbqopr.cn

Zhù zhǐ: Chí Jì Míng Guǎngxī Zhuàngzú Zìzhìqū Nánníng Shì Mǎ Shānxiàn Tiě Huán Lù 425 Hào Sì Guàn Gōng Yù 5 Céng 955 Shì (Yóuzhèng Biānmǎ：568160). Liánxì Diànhuà：40421249. Diànzǐ Yóuxiāng：qovme@aicbqopr.cn

Ji Ming Chi, Room# 955, Floor# 5, Si Guan Apartment, 425 Tie Huan Road, Mashan County, NanNing, Guangxi Autonomous Region. Postal Code: 568160. Phone Number：40421249. E-mail：qovme@aicbqopr.cn

902。姓名: 荆辉大

住址（公司）：广西壮族自治区贺州市昭平县员盛路 608 号甫锡有限公司（邮政编码：432698）。联系电话：82250736。电子邮箱：fahni@lpzyoefr.biz.cn

Zhù zhǐ: Jīng Huī Dài Guǎngxī Zhuàngzú Zìzhìqū Hèzhōu Shì Zhāopíng Xiàn Yún Shèng Lù 608 Hào Fú Xī Yǒuxiàn Gōngsī (Yóuzhèng Biānmǎ：432698). Liánxì Diànhuà：82250736. Diànzǐ Yóuxiāng：fahni@lpzyoefr.biz.cn

Hui Dai Jing, Fu Xi Corporation, 608 Yun Sheng Road, Zhaoping County, Hezhou, Guangxi Autonomous Region. Postal Code: 432698. Phone Number：82250736. E-mail：fahni@lpzyoefr.biz.cn

903。姓名: 尚坡隆

住址（机场）：广西壮族自治区玉林市博白县德顺路 210 号玉林源鸣国际机场（邮政编码：953152）。联系电话：79874237。电子邮箱：hksjw@matqnckj.airports.cn

Zhù zhǐ: Shàng Pō Lóng Guǎngxī Zhuàngzú Zìzhìqū Yùlín Shì Bó Bái Xiàn Dé Shùn Lù 210 Hào Yùlín Yuán Míng Guó Jì Jī Chǎng (Yóuzhèng Biānmǎ：953152). Liánxì Diànhuà：79874237. Diànzǐ Yóuxiāng：hksjw@matqnckj.airports.cn

Po Long Shang, Yulin Yuan Ming International Airport, 210 De Shun Road, Bobai County, Yulin, Guangxi Autonomous Region. Postal Code: 953152. Phone Number：79874237. E-mail：hksjw@matqnckj.airports.cn

904。姓名: 阎柱民

住址（公司）：广西壮族自治区柳州市融安县大庆路 635 号际启有限公司（邮政编码：959385）。联系电话：49779138。电子邮箱：rkdhv@uhodeiqt.biz.cn

Zhù zhǐ: Yán Zhù Mín Guǎngxī Zhuàngzú Zìzhìqū Liǔzhōu Shì Róng Ānxiàn Dà Qìng Lù 635 Hào Jì Qǐ Yǒuxiàn Gōngsī (Yóuzhèng Biānmǎ：959385). Liánxì Diànhuà：49779138. Diànzǐ Yóuxiāng：rkdhv@uhodeiqt.biz.cn

Zhu Min Yan, Ji Qi Corporation, 635 Da Qing Road, Rongan County, Liuzhou, Guangxi Autonomous Region. Postal Code: 959385. Phone Number：49779138. E-mail：rkdhv@uhodeiqt.biz.cn

905。姓名: 隆葛锤

住址（家庭）：广西壮族自治区崇左市天等县楚乙路 123 号盛陆公寓 39 层 239 室（邮政编码：856971）。联系电话：16826940。电子邮箱：kuslr@prkisjtx.cn

Zhù zhǐ: Lóng Gé Chuí Guǎngxī Zhuàngzú Zìzhìqū Chóng Zuǒ Shì Tiān Děng Xiàn Chǔ Yǐ Lù 123 Hào Chéng Liù Gōng Yù 39 Céng 239 Shì (Yóuzhèng Biānmǎ：856971). Liánxì Diànhuà： 16826940. Diànzǐ Yóuxiāng： kuslr@prkisjtx.cn

Ge Chui Long, Room# 239, Floor# 39, Cheng Liu Apartment, 123 Chu Yi Road, Tiandeng County, Chongzuo, Guangxi Autonomous Region. Postal Code: 856971. Phone Number： 16826940. E-mail： kuslr@prkisjtx.cn

906。姓名: 祖浩隆

住址（公园）：广西壮族自治区钦州市灵山县土智路 458 号不骥公园（邮政编码：540591）。联系电话：90691930。电子邮箱：yuabm@knhbiefs.parks.cn

Zhù zhǐ: Zǔ Hào Lóng Guǎngxī Zhuàngzú Zìzhìqū Qīnzhōu Shì Língshān Xiàn Tǔ Zhì Lù 458 Hào Bù Jì Gōng Yuán (Yóuzhèng Biānmǎ：540591). Liánxì Diànhuà： 90691930. Diànzǐ Yóuxiāng： yuabm@knhbiefs.parks.cn

Hao Long Zu, Bu Ji Park, 458 Tu Zhi Road, Lingshan County, Qinzhou, Guangxi Autonomous Region. Postal Code: 540591. Phone Number： 90691930. E-mail： yuabm@knhbiefs.parks.cn

907。姓名: 任钦亚

住址（机场）：广西壮族自治区柳州市城中区食黎路 653 号柳州俊山国际机场（邮政编码：911054）。联系电话：75798244。电子邮箱：wqelg@shntpwqg.airports.cn

Zhù zhǐ: Rèn Qīn Yà Guǎngxī Zhuàngzú Zìzhìqū Liǔzhōu Shì Chéngzhōng Qū Sì Lí Lù 653 Hào Liǔzōu Jùn Shān Guó Jì Jī Chǎng (Yóuzhèng Biānmǎ: 911054). Liánxì Diànhuà: 75798244. Diànzǐ Yóuxiāng: wqelg@shntpwqg.airports.cn

Qin Ya Ren, Liuzhou Jun Shan International Airport, 653 Si Li Road, Chengzhong District, Liuzhou, Guangxi Autonomous Region. Postal Code: 911054. Phone Number: 75798244. E-mail: wqelg@shntpwqg.airports.cn

908。姓名: 郭兆洵

住址（酒店）：广西壮族自治区防城港市港口区迅寰路 559 号近帆酒店（邮政编码：864487）。联系电话：16832368。电子邮箱：exlzd@hjkomsyl.biz.cn

Zhù zhǐ: Guō Zhào Xún Guǎngxī Zhuàngzú Zìzhìqū Fángchénggǎng Shì Gǎngkǒu Qū Xùn Huán Lù 559 Hào Jìn Fān Jiǔ Diàn (Yóuzhèng Biānmǎ: 864487). Liánxì Diànhuà: 16832368. Diànzǐ Yóuxiāng: exlzd@hjkomsyl.biz.cn

Zhao Xun Guo, Jin Fan Hotel, 559 Xun Huan Road, Port Area, Fangchenggang, Guangxi Autonomous Region. Postal Code: 864487. Phone Number: 16832368. E-mail: exlzd@hjkomsyl.biz.cn

909。姓名: 慕容迅嘉

住址（公园）：广西壮族自治区钦州市钦北区迅伦路 711 号钦珂公园（邮政编码：783747）。联系电话：61765243。电子邮箱：wbpei@phdqersa.parks.cn

Zhù zhǐ: Mùróng Xùn Jiā Guǎngxī Zhuàngzú Zìzhìqū Qīnzhōu Shì Qīn Běi Qū Xùn Lún Lù 711 Hào Qīn Kē Gōng Yuán (Yóuzhèng Biānmǎ: 783747). Liánxì Diànhuà: 61765243. Diànzǐ Yóuxiāng: wbpei@phdqersa.parks.cn

Xun Jia Murong, Qin Ke Park, 711 Xun Lun Road, Qinbei District, Qinzhou, Guangxi Autonomous Region. Postal Code: 783747. Phone Number: 61765243. E-mail: wbpei@phdqersa.parks.cn

910。姓名: 阴铭化

住址（公园）：广西壮族自治区玉林市容县浩石路 458 号强铭公园（邮政编码：575053）。联系电话：73816687。电子邮箱：huldv@toszudjg.parks.cn

Zhù zhǐ: Yīn Míng Huà Guǎngxī Zhuàngzú Zìzhìqū Yùlín Shì Róngxiàn Hào Shí Lù 458 Hào Qiǎng Míng Gōng Yuán（Yóuzhèng Biānmǎ：575053). Liánxì Diànhuà：73816687. Diànzǐ Yóuxiāng：huldv@toszudjg.parks.cn

Ming Hua Yin, Qiang Ming Park, 458 Hao Shi Road, Rong County, Yulin, Guangxi Autonomous Region. Postal Code: 575053. Phone Number：73816687. E-mail：huldv@toszudjg.parks.cn

911。姓名: 居食威

住址（机场）：广西壮族自治区来宾市兴宾区南际路 528 号来宾宝臻国际机场（邮政编码：598250）。联系电话：43769856。电子邮箱：juqkc@nguhyrza.airports.cn

Zhù zhǐ: Jū Sì Wēi Guǎngxī Zhuàngzú Zìzhìqū Láibīn Shì Xìng Bīn Qū Nán Jì Lù 528 Hào Láibīn Bǎo Zhēn Guó Jì Jī Chǎng（Yóuzhèng Biānmǎ：598250). Liánxì Diànhuà：43769856. Diànzǐ Yóuxiāng：juqkc@nguhyrza.airports.cn

Si Wei Ju, Laibin Bao Zhen International Airport, 528 Nan Ji Road, Xingbin District, Laibin, Guangxi Autonomous Region. Postal Code: 598250. Phone Number：43769856. E-mail：juqkc@nguhyrza.airports.cn

912。姓名: 邰兵陶

住址（机场）：广西壮族自治区百色市乐业县奎澜路 419 号百色世斌国际机场（邮政编码：909216）。联系电话：30210979。电子邮箱：lispk@vshgxeam.airports.cn

Zhù zhǐ: Tái Bīng Táo Guǎngxī Zhuàngzú Zìzhìqū Bǎisè Shì Lè Yè Xiàn Kuí Lán Lù 419 Hào Bǎisè Shì Bīn Guó Jì Jī Chǎng（Yóuzhèng Biānmǎ：909216). Liánxì Diànhuà：30210979. Diànzǐ Yóuxiāng：lispk@vshgxeam.airports.cn

Bing Tao Tai, Baise Shi Bin International Airport, 419 Kui Lan Road, Leye County, Baise, Guangxi Autonomous Region. Postal Code: 909216. Phone Number：30210979. E-mail：lispk@vshgxeam.airports.cn

913。姓名: 詹秀可

住址（广场）：广西壮族自治区梧州市龙圩区晖盛路 452 号员汉广场（邮政编码：598441）。联系电话：66465584。电子邮箱：erkag@nrmxjiyv.squares.cn

Zhù zhǐ: Zhān Xiù Kě Guǎngxī Zhuàngzú Zìzhìqū Wúzhōu Shì Lóng Wéi Qū Huī Shèng Lù 452 Hào Yuán Hàn Guǎng Chǎng（Yóuzhèng Biānmǎ：598441). Liánxì Diànhuà：66465584. Diànzǐ Yóuxiāng：erkag@nrmxjiyv.squares.cn

Xiu Ke Zhan, Yuan Han Square, 452 Hui Sheng Road, Longxu District, Wuzhou, Guangxi Autonomous Region. Postal Code: 598441. Phone Number：66465584. E-mail：erkag@nrmxjiyv.squares.cn

914。姓名: 能成宝

住址（寺庙）：广西壮族自治区贺州市八步区己守路 505 号己舟寺（邮政编码：583328）。联系电话：47623897。电子邮箱：cizye@uqhjsxvk.god.cn

Zhù zhǐ: Nài Chéng Bǎo Guǎngxī Zhuàngzú Zìzhìqū Hèzhōu Shì Bā Bù Qū Jǐ Shǒu Lù 505 Hào Jǐ Zhōu Sì（Yóuzhèng Biānmǎ：583328). Liánxì Diànhuà：47623897. Diànzǐ Yóuxiāng：cizye@uqhjsxvk.god.cn

Cheng Bao Nai, Ji Zhou Temple, 505 Ji Shou Road, Babu District, Hezhou, Guangxi Autonomous Region. Postal Code: 583328. Phone Number：47623897. E-mail：cizye@uqhjsxvk.god.cn

915。姓名: 卜自征

住址（公共汽车站）：广西壮族自治区柳州市柳南区中珏路 384 号豹岐站（邮政编码：249910）。联系电话：32804092。电子邮箱：dnlhm@fuohlzsa.transport.cn

Zhù zhǐ: Bǔ Zì Zhēng Guǎngxī Zhuàngzú Zìzhìqū Liǔzhōu Shì Liǔ Nán Qū Zhòng Jué Lù 384 Hào Bào Qí Zhàn（Yóuzhèng Biānmǎ：249910). Liánxì Diànhuà：32804092. Diànzǐ Yóuxiāng：dnlhm@fuohlzsa.transport.cn

Zi Zheng Bu, Bao Qi Bus Station, 384 Zhong Jue Road, Liunan District, Liuzhou, Guangxi Autonomous Region. Postal Code: 249910. Phone Number：32804092. E-mail：dnlhm@fuohlzsa.transport.cn

916。姓名: 荆彬中

住址（公园）：广西壮族自治区梧州市藤县豹进路 590 号钢员公园（邮政编码：965452）。联系电话：94161589。电子邮箱：dztyf@mrjptsaq.parks.cn

Zhù zhǐ: Jīng Bīn Zhòng Guǎngxī Zhuàngzú Zìzhìqū Wúzhōu Shì Téng Xiàn Bào Jìn Lù 590 Hào Gāng Yuán Gōng Yuán（Yóuzhèng Biānmǎ：965452). Liánxì Diànhuà：94161589. Diànzǐ Yóuxiāng：dztyf@mrjptsaq.parks.cn

Bin Zhong Jing, Gang Yuan Park, 590 Bao Jin Road, Fuji County, Wuzhou, Guangxi Autonomous Region. Postal Code: 965452. Phone Number：94161589. E-mail：dztyf@mrjptsaq.parks.cn

917。姓名: 韶盛焯

住址（酒店）：广西壮族自治区钦州市钦南区宝山路 988 号亭易酒店（邮政编码：357238）。联系电话：34475591。电子邮箱：yqrxu@tdpsgcwf.biz.cn

Zhù zhǐ: Sháo Chéng Chāo Guǎngxī Zhuàngzú Zìzhìqū Qīnzhōu Shì Qīn Nán Qū Bǎo Shān Lù 988 Hào Tíng Yì Jiǔ Diàn（Yóuzhèng Biānmǎ：357238). Liánxì Diànhuà：34475591. Diànzǐ Yóuxiāng：yqrxu@tdpsgcwf.biz.cn

Cheng Chao Shao, Ting Yi Hotel, 988 Bao Shan Road, Chennan District, Qinzhou, Guangxi Autonomous Region. Postal Code: 357238. Phone Number：34475591. E-mail：yqrxu@tdpsgcwf.biz.cn

918。姓名: 东焯臻

住址（医院）：广西壮族自治区崇左市江州区顺阳路 475 号轶食医院（邮政编码：459928）。联系电话：51198878。电子邮箱：oajfr@oiqmpkzy.health.cn

Zhù zhǐ: Dōng Zhuō Zhēn Guǎngxī Zhuàngzú Zìzhìqū Chóng Zuǒ Shì Jiāng Zhōu Qū Shùn Yáng Lù 475 Hào Yì Shí Yī Yuàn (Yóuzhèng Biānmǎ：459928). Liánxì Diànhuà：51198878. Diànzǐ Yóuxiāng：oajfr@oiqmpkzy.health.cn

Zhuo Zhen Dong, Yi Shi Hospital, 475 Shun Yang Road, Jiangzhou District, Chongzuo, Guangxi Autonomous Region. Postal Code: 459928. Phone Number：51198878. E-mail：oajfr@oiqmpkzy.health.cn

919。姓名: 穆刚轼

住址（公司）：广西壮族自治区百色市平果市可圣路 940 号仓中有限公司（邮政编码：964511）。联系电话：68469063。电子邮箱：zkeyp@pagevwtj.biz.cn

Zhù zhǐ: Mù Gāng Shì Guǎngxī Zhuàngzú Zìzhìqū Bǎisè Shì Píng Guǒ Shì Kě Shèng Lù 940 Hào Cāng Zhòng Yǒuxiàn Gōngsī (Yóuzhèng Biānmǎ：964511). Liánxì Diànhuà：68469063. Diànzǐ Yóuxiāng：zkeyp@pagevwtj.biz.cn

Gang Shi Mu, Cang Zhong Corporation, 940 Ke Sheng Road, Pingguo City, Baise, Guangxi Autonomous Region. Postal Code: 964511. Phone Number：68469063. E-mail：zkeyp@pagevwtj.biz.cn

920。姓名: 卓歧坡

住址（酒店）：广西壮族自治区河池市凤山县员葆路 978 号舟沛酒店（邮政编码：272817）。联系电话：34465445。电子邮箱：onjds@awhcyqei.biz.cn

Zhù zhǐ: Zhuó Qí Pō Guǎngxī Zhuàngzú Zìzhìqū Héchí Shì Fèng Shān Xiàn Yún Bǎo Lù 978 Hào Zhōu Bèi Jiǔ Diàn (Yóuzhèng Biānmǎ：272817). Liánxì Diànhuà：34465445. Diànzǐ Yóuxiāng：onjds@awhcyqei.biz.cn

Qi Po Zhuo, Zhou Bei Hotel, 978 Yun Bao Road, Fengshan County, Hechi, Guangxi Autonomous Region. Postal Code: 272817. Phone Number：34465445. E-mail：onjds@awhcyqei.biz.cn

921。姓名: 左斌乐

住址（公共汽车站）：广西壮族自治区百色市那坡县钦克路 393 号伦继站（邮政编码：464931）。联系电话：59478790。电子邮箱：kpeml@harxutnq.transport.cn

Zhù zhǐ: Zuǒ Bīn Lè Guǎngxī Zhuàngzú Zìzhìqū Bǎisè Shì Nà Pō Xiàn Qīn Kè Lù 393 Hào Lún Jì Zhàn (Yóuzhèng Biānmǎ：464931). Liánxì Diànhuà：59478790. Diànzǐ Yóuxiāng：kpeml@harxutnq.transport.cn

Bin Le Zuo, Lun Ji Bus Station, 393 Qin Ke Road, Napo County, Baise, Guangxi Autonomous Region. Postal Code: 464931. Phone Number：59478790. E-mail：kpeml@harxutnq.transport.cn

922。姓名: 申食计

住址（湖泊）：广西壮族自治区来宾市金秀瑶族自治县化刚路 902 号来金湖（邮政编码：746091）。联系电话：51665804。电子邮箱：gujxp@zrugfwjx.lakes.cn

Zhù zhǐ: Shēn Yì Jì Guǎngxī Zhuàngzú Zìzhìqū Láibīn Shì Jīn Xiù Yáozú Zìzhìxiàn Huā Gāng Lù 902 Hào Lái Jīn Hú (Yóuzhèng Biānmǎ：746091). Liánxì Diànhuà：51665804. Diànzǐ Yóuxiāng：gujxp@zrugfwjx.lakes.cn

Yi Ji Shen, Lai Jin Lake, 902 Hua Gang Road, Jinxiu Yao Autonomous County, Laibin, Guangxi Autonomous Region. Postal Code: 746091. Phone Number：51665804. E-mail：gujxp@zrugfwjx.lakes.cn

923。姓名:淳于中庆

住址（湖泊）：广西壮族自治区梧州市岑溪市桥队路 389 号淹来湖（邮政编码：394287）。联系电话：41878433。电子邮箱：scxwq@qwlnkeis.lakes.cn

Zhù zhǐ: Chúnyú Zhòng Qìng Guǎngxī Zhuàngzú Zìzhìqū Wúzhōu Shì Cénxī Shì Qiáo Duì Lù 389 Hào Yān Lái Hú (Yóuzhèng Biānmǎ: 394287). Liánxì Diànhuà: 41878433. Diànzǐ Yóuxiāng: scxwq@qwlnkeis.lakes.cn

Zhong Qing Chunyu, Yan Lai Lake, 389 Qiao Dui Road, Cenxi City, Wuzhou, Guangxi Autonomous Region. Postal Code: 394287. Phone Number: 41878433. E-mail: scxwq@qwlnkeis.lakes.cn

924。姓名: 方隆鹤

住址（公司）：广西壮族自治区柳州市柳北区维骥路 521 号民涛有限公司（邮政编码：272863）。联系电话：47465459。电子邮箱：udzyt@yhptzwrx.biz.cn

Zhù zhǐ: Fāng Lóng Hè Guǎngxī Zhuàngzú Zìzhìqū Liǔzhōu Shì Liǔběi Qū Wéi Jì Lù 521 Hào Mín Tāo Yǒuxiàn Gōngsī (Yóuzhèng Biānmǎ: 272863). Liánxì Diànhuà: 47465459. Diànzǐ Yóuxiāng: udzyt@yhptzwrx.biz.cn

Long He Fang, Min Tao Corporation, 521 Wei Ji Road, Liubei District, Liuzhou, Guangxi Autonomous Region. Postal Code: 272863. Phone Number: 47465459. E-mail: udzyt@yhptzwrx.biz.cn

925。姓名: 寿迅锤

住址（公共汽车站）：广西壮族自治区梧州市岑溪市焯智路 915 号九先站（邮政编码：965991）。联系电话：30121608。电子邮箱：quywa@otgjplzn.transport.cn

Zhù zhǐ: Shòu Xùn Chuí Guǎngxī Zhuàngzú Zìzhìqū Wúzhōu Shì Cénxī Shì Zhuō Zhì Lù 915 Hào Jiǔ Xiān Zhàn (Yóuzhèng Biānmǎ: 965991). Liánxì Diànhuà: 30121608. Diànzǐ Yóuxiāng: quywa@otgjplzn.transport.cn

Xun Chui Shou, Jiu Xian Bus Station, 915 Zhuo Zhi Road, Cenxi City, Wuzhou, Guangxi Autonomous Region. Postal Code: 965991. Phone Number: 30121608. E-mail: quywa@otgjplzn.transport.cn

926。姓名: 南宫国伦

住址（机场）：广西壮族自治区北海市海城区恩克路 946 号北海祥舟国际机场（邮政编码：279186）。联系电话：82734261。电子邮箱：foiqb@nyarfvux.airports.cn

Zhù zhǐ: Nángōng Guó Lún Guǎngxī Zhuàngzú Zìzhìqū Běihǎi Shì Hǎi Chéngqū Ēn Kè Lù 946 Hào Běiǎi Xiáng Zhōu Guó Jì Jī Chǎng （Yóuzhèng Biānmǎ：279186). Liánxì Diànhuà：82734261. Diànzǐ Yóuxiāng：foiqb@nyarfvux.airports.cn

Guo Lun Nangong, Beihai Xiang Zhou International Airport, 946 En Ke Road, Haicheng District, Beihai, Guangxi Autonomous Region. Postal Code: 279186. Phone Number：82734261. E-mail：foiqb@nyarfvux.airports.cn

927。姓名: 暨食祥

住址（寺庙）：广西壮族自治区贺州市昭平县黎伦路 286 号葆中寺（邮政编码：450139）。联系电话：62562673。电子邮箱：rlwzv@fyqbpmwi.god.cn

Zhù zhǐ: Jì Shí Xiáng Guǎngxī Zhuàngzú Zìzhìqū Hèzhōu Shì Zhāopíng Xiàn Lí Lún Lù 286 Hào Bǎo Zhòng Sì （Yóuzhèng Biānmǎ：450139). Liánxì Diànhuà：62562673. Diànzǐ Yóuxiāng：rlwzv@fyqbpmwi.god.cn

Shi Xiang Ji, Bao Zhong Temple, 286 Li Lun Road, Zhaoping County, Hezhou, Guangxi Autonomous Region. Postal Code: 450139. Phone Number：62562673. E-mail：rlwzv@fyqbpmwi.god.cn

928。姓名: 糜居钢

住址（公司）：广西壮族自治区南宁市武鸣区仓来路 552 号仓迅有限公司（邮政编码：374404）。联系电话：35217771。电子邮箱：kclxu@xengviyk.biz.cn

Zhù zhǐ: Mí Jū Gāng Guǎngxī Zhuàngzú Zìzhìqū Nánníng Shì Wǔ Míng Qū Cāng Lái Lù 552 Hào Cāng Xùn Yǒuxiàn Gōngsī （Yóuzhèng Biānmǎ：374404). Liánxì Diànhuà：35217771. Diànzǐ Yóuxiāng：kclxu@xengviyk.biz.cn

Ju Gang Mi, Cang Xun Corporation, 552 Cang Lai Road, Wuming District, NanNing, Guangxi Autonomous Region. Postal Code: 374404. Phone Number：35217771. E-mail：kclxu@xengviyk.biz.cn

929。姓名: 邓秀仲

住址（大学）：广西壮族自治区钦州市钦南区立辉大学轶近路 269 号（邮政编码：911561）。联系电话：55447962。电子邮箱：kezvt@iourfzqm.edu.cn

Zhù zhǐ: Dèng Xiù Zhòng Guǎngxī Zhuàngzú Zìzhìqū Qīnzhōu Shì Qīn Nán Qū Lì Huī DàxuéYì Jìn Lù 269 Hào (Yóuzhèng Biānmǎ：911561). Liánxì Diànhuà：55447962. Diànzǐ Yóuxiāng：kezvt@iourfzqm.edu.cn

Xiu Zhong Deng, Li Hui University, 269 Yi Jin Road, Chennan District, Qinzhou, Guangxi Autonomous Region. Postal Code: 911561. Phone Number：55447962. E-mail：kezvt@iourfzqm.edu.cn

930。姓名: 许焯阳

住址（公共汽车站）：广西壮族自治区来宾市兴宾区舟寰路 256 号黎征站（邮政编码：585018）。联系电话：80243308。电子邮箱：cakyp@qnskagzr.transport.cn

Zhù zhǐ: Xǔ Zhuō Yáng Guǎngxī Zhuàngzú Zìzhìqū Láibīn Shì Xìng Bīn Qū Zhōu Huán Lù 256 Hào Lí Zhēng Zhàn (Yóuzhèng Biānmǎ：585018). Liánxì Diànhuà：80243308. Diànzǐ Yóuxiāng：cakyp@qnskagzr.transport.cn

Zhuo Yang Xu, Li Zheng Bus Station, 256 Zhou Huan Road, Xingbin District, Laibin, Guangxi Autonomous Region. Postal Code: 585018. Phone Number：80243308. E-mail：cakyp@qnskagzr.transport.cn

931。姓名: 云征隆

住址（寺庙）：广西壮族自治区北海市银海区迅德路 352 号先圣寺（邮政编码：973962）。联系电话：93733818。电子邮箱：fbwju@fslxeugk.god.cn

Zhù zhǐ: Yún Zhēng Lóng Guǎngxī Zhuàngzú Zìzhìqū Běihǎi Shì Yín Hǎi Qū Xùn Dé Lù 352 Hào Xiān Shèng Sì (Yóuzhèng Biānmǎ：973962). Liánxì Diànhuà: 93733818. Diànzǐ Yóuxiāng：fbwju@fslxeugk.god.cn

Zheng Long Yun, Xian Sheng Temple, 352 Xun De Road, Yinhai District, Beihai, Guangxi Autonomous Region. Postal Code: 973962. Phone Number：93733818. E-mail：fbwju@fslxeugk.god.cn

932。姓名: 包毅可

住址（酒店）：广西壮族自治区来宾市金秀瑶族自治县澜磊路 758 号骥坚酒店（邮政编码：630619）。联系电话：17838660。电子邮箱：gaike@sfkgqnxu.biz.cn

Zhù zhǐ: Bāo Yì Kě Guǎngxī Zhuàngzú Zìzhìqū Láibīn Shì Jīn Xiù Yáozú Zìzhìxiàn Lán Lěi Lù 758 Hào Jì Jiān Jiǔ Diàn (Yóuzhèng Biānmǎ：630619). Liánxì Diànhuà: 17838660. Diànzǐ Yóuxiāng：gaike@sfkgqnxu.biz.cn

Yi Ke Bao, Ji Jian Hotel, 758 Lan Lei Road, Jinxiu Yao Autonomous County, Laibin, Guangxi Autonomous Region. Postal Code: 630619. Phone Number：17838660. E-mail：gaike@sfkgqnxu.biz.cn

933。姓名: 李伦臻

住址（机场）：广西壮族自治区崇左市天等县沛食路 198 号崇左红骥国际机场（邮政编码：884385）。联系电话：92154568。电子邮箱：ouwml@swotylux.airports.cn

Zhù zhǐ: Lǐ Lún Zhēn Guǎngxī Zhuàngzú Zìzhìqū Chóng Zuǒ Shì Tiān Děng Xiàn Pèi Shí Lù 198 Hào Cóng Zuǒ Hóng Jì Guó Jì Jī Chǎng （Yóuzhèng Biānmǎ：884385）. Liánxì Diànhuà：92154568. Diànzǐ Yóuxiāng：ouwml@swotylux.airports.cn

Lun Zhen Li, Chongzuo Hong Ji International Airport, 198 Pei Shi Road, Tiandeng County, Chongzuo, Guangxi Autonomous Region. Postal Code: 884385. Phone Number：92154568. E-mail：ouwml@swotylux.airports.cn

934。姓名: 郁陆庆

住址（湖泊）：广西壮族自治区北海市合浦县龙涛路 446 号渊澜湖（邮政编码：984531）。联系电话：71699929。电子邮箱：gdqfo@aktscxeo.lakes.cn

Zhù zhǐ: Yù Liù Qìng Guǎngxī Zhuàngzú Zìzhìqū Běihǎi Shì Hépǔ Xiàn Lóng Tāo Lù 446 Hào Yuān Lán Hú （Yóuzhèng Biānmǎ：984531). Liánxì Diànhuà：71699929. Diànzǐ Yóuxiāng：gdqfo@aktscxeo.lakes.cn

Liu Qing Yu, Yuan Lan Lake, 446 Long Tao Road, Hepu County, Beihai, Guangxi Autonomous Region. Postal Code: 984531. Phone Number：71699929. E-mail：gdqfo@aktscxeo.lakes.cn

935。姓名: 阮翰亮

住址（酒店）：广西壮族自治区柳州市三江侗族自治县阳豪路 158 号不中酒店（邮政编码：393698）。联系电话：46254699。电子邮箱：rlkhy@hdofapzc.biz.cn

Zhù zhǐ: Ruǎn Hàn Liàng Guǎngxī Zhuàngzú Zìzhìqū Liǔzhōu Shì Sānjiāng Dòngzú Zìzhìxiàn Yáng Háo Lù 158 Hào Bù Zhòng Jiǔ Diàn （Yóuzhèng Biānmǎ：393698). Liánxì Diànhuà：46254699. Diànzǐ Yóuxiāng：rlkhy@hdofapzc.biz.cn

Han Liang Ruan, Bu Zhong Hotel, 158 Yang Hao Road, Sanjiang Dong Autonomous County, Liuzhou, Guangxi Autonomous Region. Postal Code: 393698. Phone Number：46254699. E-mail：rlkhy@hdofapzc.biz.cn

936。姓名: 公羊帆水

住址（医院）：广西壮族自治区梧州市龙圩区豪磊路 872 号世陆医院（邮政编码：605254）。联系电话：83050886。电子邮箱：kqfyj@trzwjace.health.cn

Zhù zhǐ: Gōngyáng Fān Shuǐ Guǎngxī Zhuàngzú Zìzhìqū Wúzhōu Shì Lóng Wéi Qū Háo Lěi Lù 872 Hào Shì Lù Yī Yuàn（Yóuzhèng Biānmǎ：605254). Liánxì Diànhuà：83050886. Diànzǐ Yóuxiāng：kqfyj@trzwjace.health.cn

Fan Shui Gongyang, Shi Lu Hospital, 872 Hao Lei Road, Longxu District, Wuzhou, Guangxi Autonomous Region. Postal Code: 605254. Phone Number：83050886. E-mail：kqfyj@trzwjace.health.cn

937。姓名: 郦钊钢

住址（公共汽车站）：广西壮族自治区南宁市宾阳县宽乐路 568 号铁立站（邮政编码：744805）。联系电话：93458983。电子邮箱：kfuqj@mbvegilu.transport.cn

Zhù zhǐ: Lì Zhāo Gāng Guǎngxī Zhuàngzú Zìzhìqū Nánníng Shì Bīn Yáng Xiàn Kuān Lè Lù 568 Hào Tiě Lì Zhàn（Yóuzhèng Biānmǎ：744805). Liánxì Diànhuà：93458983. Diànzǐ Yóuxiāng：kfuqj@mbvegilu.transport.cn

Zhao Gang Li, Tie Li Bus Station, 568 Kuan Le Road, Binyang County, NanNing, Guangxi Autonomous Region. Postal Code: 744805. Phone Number：93458983. E-mail：kfuqj@mbvegilu.transport.cn

938。姓名: 阮迅土

住址（公共汽车站）：广西壮族自治区贺州市富川瑶族自治县九仲路 591 号石际站（邮政编码：296664）。联系电话：50177617。电子邮箱：mpyko@cewaityk.transport.cn

Zhù zhǐ: Ruǎn Xùn Tǔ Guǎngxī Zhuàngzú Zìzhìqū Hèzhōu Shì Fùchuān Yáozú Zìzhìxiàn Jiǔ Zhòng Lù 591 Hào Shí Jì Zhàn（Yóuzhèng Biānmǎ：296664). Liánxì Diànhuà：50177617. Diànzǐ Yóuxiāng：mpyko@cewaityk.transport.cn

Xun Tu Ruan, Shi Ji Bus Station, 591 Jiu Zhong Road, Fuchuan Yao Autonomous County, Hezhou, Guangxi Autonomous Region. Postal Code: 296664. Phone Number：50177617. E-mail：mpyko@cewaityk.transport.cn

939。姓名: 秦寰成

住址（机场）：广西壮族自治区贺州市昭平县人石路 282 号贺州谢己国际机场（邮政编码：961221）。联系电话：71871302。电子邮箱：ivnfu@vmnfzwsy.airports.cn

Zhù zhǐ: Qín Huán Chéng Guǎngxī Zhuàngzú Zìzhìqū Hèzhōu Shì Zhāopíng Xiàn Rén Shí Lù 282 Hào Hèzōu Xiè Jǐ Guó Jì Jī Chǎng (Yóuzhèng Biānmǎ： 961221). Liánxì Diànhuà： 71871302. Diànzǐ Yóuxiāng： ivnfu@vmnfzwsy.airports.cn

Huan Cheng Qin, Hezhou Xie Ji International Airport, 282 Ren Shi Road, Zhaoping County, Hezhou, Guangxi Autonomous Region. Postal Code: 961221. Phone Number：71871302. E-mail：ivnfu@vmnfzwsy.airports.cn

940。姓名: 葛中世

住址（火车站）：广西壮族自治区梧州市万秀区乙淹路 748 号梧州站（邮政编码：493902）。联系电话：12531537。电子邮箱：yqwlx@hvkrayin.chr.cn

Zhù zhǐ: Gě Zhōng Shì Guǎngxī Zhuàngzú Zìzhìqū Wúzhōu Shì Wàn Xiù Qū Yǐ Yān Lù 748 Hào Wúzōu Zhàn (Yóuzhèng Biānmǎ：493902). Liánxì Diànhuà： 12531537. Diànzǐ Yóuxiāng： yqwlx@hvkrayin.chr.cn

Zhong Shi Ge, Wuzhou Railway Station, 748 Yi Yan Road, Wanxiu District, Wuzhou, Guangxi Autonomous Region. Postal Code: 493902. Phone Number：12531537. E-mail：yqwlx@hvkrayin.chr.cn

941。姓名: 赖阳亮

住址（大学）：广西壮族自治区来宾市兴宾区水院大学振食路 811 号（邮政编码：316088）。联系电话：31872836。电子邮箱：huqkl@anrqgumo.edu.cn

Zhù zhǐ: Lài Yáng Liàng Guǎngxī Zhuàngzú Zìzhìqū Láibīn Shì Xìng Bīn Qū Shuǐ Yuàn DàxuéZhèn Sì Lù 811 Hào（Yóuzhèng Biānmǎ：316088）. Liánxì Diànhuà：31872836. Diànzǐ Yóuxiāng：huqkl@anrqgumo.edu.cn

Yang Liang Lai, Shui Yuan University, 811 Zhen Si Road, Xingbin District, Laibin, Guangxi Autonomous Region. Postal Code: 316088. Phone Number：31872836. E-mail：huqkl@anrqgumo.edu.cn

942。姓名: 都大跃

住址（大学）：广西壮族自治区河池市大化瑶族自治县铭坡大学克胜路 341 号（邮政编码：404452）。联系电话：32658878。电子邮箱：yvwho@edhrptnq.edu.cn

Zhù zhǐ: Dū Dài Yuè Guǎngxī Zhuàngzú Zìzhìqū Héchí Shì Dà Huà Yáozú Zìzhìxiàn Míng Pō DàxuéKè Shēng Lù 341 Hào（Yóuzhèng Biānmǎ：404452). Liánxì Diànhuà：32658878. Diànzǐ Yóuxiāng：yvwho@edhrptnq.edu.cn

Dai Yue Du, Ming Po University, 341 Ke Sheng Road, Dahua Yao Autonomous County, Hechi, Guangxi Autonomous Region. Postal Code: 404452. Phone Number：32658878. E-mail：yvwho@edhrptnq.edu.cn

943。姓名: 慕柱民

住址（家庭）：广西壮族自治区崇左市江州区先龙路 396 号乐食公寓 8 层 666 室（邮政编码：405722）。联系电话：93092808。电子邮箱：qojvf@tufhwroj.cn

Zhù zhǐ: Mù Zhù Mín Guǎngxī Zhuàngzú Zìzhìqū Chóng Zuǒ Shì Jiāng Zhōu Qū Xiān Lóng Lù 396 Hào Lè Sì Gōng Yù 8 Céng 666 Shì（Yóuzhèng Biānmǎ：405722). Liánxì Diànhuà：93092808. Diànzǐ Yóuxiāng：qojvf@tufhwroj.cn

Zhu Min Mu, Room# 666, Floor# 8, Le Si Apartment, 396 Xian Long Road, Jiangzhou District, Chongzuo, Guangxi Autonomous Region. Postal Code: 405722. Phone Number：93092808. E-mail：qojvf@tufhwroj.cn

944。姓名：亓官冠陶

住址（机场）：广西壮族自治区桂林市阳朔县辙超路 772 号桂林居跃国际机场（邮政编码：205885）。联系电话：72377803。电子邮箱：tecdk@uevqpysx.airports.cn

Zhù zhǐ: Qíguān Guān Táo Guǎngxī Zhuàngzú Zìzhìqū Guìlín Shì Yángshuò Xiàn Zhé Chāo Lù 772 Hào Gulín Jū Yuè Guó Jì Jī Chǎng (Yóuzhèng Biānmǎ：205885). Liánxì Diànhuà：72377803. Diànzǐ Yóuxiāng：tecdk@uevqpysx.airports.cn

Guan Tao Qiguan, Guilin Ju Yue International Airport, 772 Zhe Chao Road, Yangshuo County, Guilin, Guangxi Autonomous Region. Postal Code: 205885. Phone Number：72377803. E-mail：tecdk@uevqpysx.airports.cn

945。姓名：贲己风

住址（机场）：广西壮族自治区柳州市城中区王斌路 433 号柳州南翰国际机场（邮政编码：853092）。联系电话：66414736。电子邮箱：fxcbs@dxypeish.airports.cn

Zhù zhǐ: Bēn Jǐ Fēng Guǎngxī Zhuàngzú Zìzhìqū Liǔzhōu Shì Chéngzhōng Qū Wàng Bīn Lù 433 Hào Liǔzōu Nán Hàn Guó Jì Jī Chǎng (Yóuzhèng Biānmǎ：853092). Liánxì Diànhuà：66414736. Diànzǐ Yóuxiāng：fxcbs@dxypeish.airports.cn

Ji Feng Ben, Liuzhou Nan Han International Airport, 433 Wang Bin Road, Chengzhong District, Liuzhou, Guangxi Autonomous Region. Postal Code: 853092. Phone Number：66414736. E-mail：fxcbs@dxypeish.airports.cn

946。姓名：公轶国

住址（机场）：广西壮族自治区贵港市覃塘区近兵路 505 号贵港克白国际机场（邮政编码：298967）。联系电话：15953185。电子邮箱：jrwdy@ealnkypt.airports.cn

Zhù zhǐ: Gōng Yì Guó Guǎngxī Zhuàngzú Zìzhìqū Guìgǎng Shì Tán Táng Qū Jìn Bīng Lù 505 Hào Gugǎng Kè Bái Guó Jì Jī Chǎng (Yóuzhèng Biānmǎ：298967). Liánxì Diànhuà：15953185. Diànzǐ Yóuxiāng：jrwdy@ealnkypt.airports.cn

Yi Guo Gong, Guigang Ke Bai International Airport, 505 Jin Bing Road, Qintang District, Guigang, Guangxi Autonomous Region. Postal Code: 298967. Phone Number：15953185. E-mail：jrwdy@ealnkypt.airports.cn

947。姓名: 韦原翼

住址（广场）：广西壮族自治区钦州市浦北县食禹路 986 号红近广场（邮政编码：712058）。联系电话：67002153。电子邮箱：tzkqs@vcdrefap.squares.cn

Zhù zhǐ: Wéi Yuán Yì Guǎngxī Zhuàngzú Zìzhìqū Qīnzhōu Shì Pǔ Běi Xiàn Sì Yǔ Lù 986 Hào Hóng Jìn Guǎng Chǎng (Yóuzhèng Biānmǎ：712058). Liánxì Diànhuà：67002153. Diànzǐ Yóuxiāng：tzkqs@vcdrefap.squares.cn

Yuan Yi Wei, Hong Jin Square, 986 Si Yu Road, Pubei County, Qinzhou, Guangxi Autonomous Region. Postal Code: 712058. Phone Number：67002153. E-mail：tzkqs@vcdrefap.squares.cn

948。姓名: 西门游红

住址（大学）：广西壮族自治区北海市银海区惟跃大学其大路 261 号（邮政编码：800101）。联系电话：85193632。电子邮箱：mytwx@pbvynruq.edu.cn

Zhù zhǐ: Xīmén Yóu Hóng Guǎngxī Zhuàngzú Zìzhìqū Běihǎi Shì Yín Hǎi Qū Wéi Yuè DàxuéQí Dài Lù 261 Hào (Yóuzhèng Biānmǎ：800101). Liánxì Diànhuà：85193632. Diànzǐ Yóuxiāng：mytwx@pbvynruq.edu.cn

You Hong Ximen, Wei Yue University, 261 Qi Dai Road, Yinhai District, Beihai, Guangxi Autonomous Region. Postal Code: 800101. Phone Number：85193632. E-mail：mytwx@pbvynruq.edu.cn

949。姓名：籍陆化

住址（博物院）：广西壮族自治区北海市银海区俊隆路 572 号北海博物馆（邮政编码：547684）。联系电话：52926624。电子邮箱：ubdke@phzfgaiv.museums.cn

Zhù zhǐ: Jí Liù Huā Guǎngxī Zhuàngzú Zìzhìqū Běihǎi Shì Yín Hǎi Qū Jùn Lóng Lù 572 Hào Běiǎi Bó Wù Guǎn（Yóuzhèng Biānmǎ：547684). Liánxì Diànhuà：52926624. Diànzǐ Yóuxiāng：ubdke@phzfgaiv.museums.cn

Liu Hua Ji, Beihai Museum, 572 Jun Long Road, Yinhai District, Beihai, Guangxi Autonomous Region. Postal Code: 547684. Phone Number：52926624. E-mail：ubdke@phzfgaiv.museums.cn

950。姓名：羊舌跃腾

住址（公园）：广西壮族自治区柳州市城中区克渊路 324 号人愈公园（邮政编码：832749）。联系电话：63502368。电子邮箱：oqhzg@mljdavcf.parks.cn

Zhù zhǐ: Yángshé Yuè Téng Guǎngxī Zhuàngzú Zìzhìqū Liǔzhōu Shì Chéngzhōng Qū Kè Yuān Lù 324 Hào Rén Yù Gōng Yuán（Yóuzhèng Biānmǎ：832749). Liánxì Diànhuà：63502368. Diànzǐ Yóuxiāng：oqhzg@mljdavcf.parks.cn

Yue Teng Yangshe, Ren Yu Park, 324 Ke Yuan Road, Chengzhong District, Liuzhou, Guangxi Autonomous Region. Postal Code: 832749. Phone Number：63502368. E-mail：oqhzg@mljdavcf.parks.cn

951。姓名：胥食水

住址（医院）：广西壮族自治区贺州市钟山县翼继路 757 号冕辙医院（邮政编码：826146）。联系电话：63077708。电子邮箱：wjrxv@ysqkfcme.health.cn

Zhù zhǐ: Xū Yì Shuǐ Guǎngxī Zhuàngzú Zìzhìqū Hèzhōu Shì Zhōng Shān Xiàn Yì Jì Lù 757 Hào Miǎn Zhé Yī Yuàn（Yóuzhèng Biānmǎ：826146）. Liánxì Diànhuà：63077708. Diànzǐ Yóuxiāng：wjrxv@ysqkfcme.health.cn

Yi Shui Xu, Mian Zhe Hospital, 757 Yi Ji Road, Zhongshan County, Hezhou, Guangxi Autonomous Region. Postal Code: 826146. Phone Number：63077708. E-mail：wjrxv@ysqkfcme.health.cn

952。姓名: 仲稼轶

住址（大学）：广西壮族自治区北海市合浦县己食大学宽屹路 244 号（邮政编码：154586）。联系电话：50892421。电子邮箱：dfczp@pgxrsbyu.edu.cn

Zhù zhǐ: Zhòng Jià Yì Guǎngxī Zhuàngzú Zìzhìqū Běihǎi Shì Hépǔ Xiàn Jǐ Shí DàxuéKuān Yì Lù 244 Hào（Yóuzhèng Biānmǎ：154586). Liánxì Diànhuà：50892421. Diànzǐ Yóuxiāng：dfczp@pgxrsbyu.edu.cn

Jia Yi Zhong, Ji Shi University, 244 Kuan Yi Road, Hepu County, Beihai, Guangxi Autonomous Region. Postal Code: 154586. Phone Number：50892421. E-mail：dfczp@pgxrsbyu.edu.cn

953。姓名: 姬可近

住址（广场）：广西壮族自治区贵港市桂平市渊俊路 755 号陶珏广场（邮政编码：620090）。联系电话：21817776。电子邮箱：xvcnz@bfkritoy.squares.cn

Zhù zhǐ: Jī Kě Jìn Guǎngxī Zhuàngzú Zìzhìqū Guìgǎng Shì Guìpíngshì Yuān Jùn Lù 755 Hào Táo Jué Guǎng Chǎng（Yóuzhèng Biānmǎ：620090). Liánxì Diànhuà：21817776. Diànzǐ Yóuxiāng：xvcnz@bfkritoy.squares.cn

Ke Jin Ji, Tao Jue Square, 755 Yuan Jun Road, Guiping, Guigang, Guangxi Autonomous Region. Postal Code: 620090. Phone Number：21817776. E-mail：xvcnz@bfkritoy.squares.cn

954。姓名: 宋威秀

住址（公司）：广西壮族自治区贺州市平桂区游敬路 819 号成乙有限公司（邮政编码：206822）。联系电话：26979846。电子邮箱：cqaxp@fxthevcj.biz.cn

Zhù zhǐ: Sòng Wēi Xiù Guǎngxī Zhuàngzú Zìzhìqū Hèzhōu Shì Píng Guì Qū Yóu Jìng Lù 819 Hào Chéng Yǐ Yǒuxiàn Gōngsī (Yóuzhèng Biānmǎ：206822). Liánxì Diànhuà：26979846. Diànzǐ Yóuxiāng：cqaxp@fxthevcj.biz.cn

Wei Xiu Song, Cheng Yi Corporation, 819 You Jing Road, Pinggui District, Hezhou, Guangxi Autonomous Region. Postal Code: 206822. Phone Number：26979846. E-mail：cqaxp@fxthevcj.biz.cn

955。姓名: 隆超汉

住址（家庭）：广西壮族自治区玉林市兴业县辙领路 694 号鹤领公寓 37 层 498 室（邮政编码：455379）。联系电话：21416784。电子邮箱：ioqch@tcwinvqf.cn

Zhù zhǐ: Lóng Chāo Hàn Guǎngxī Zhuàngzú Zìzhìqū Yùlín Shì Xìngyè Xiàn Zhé Lǐng Lù 694 Hào Hè Lǐng Gōng Yù 37 Céng 498 Shì (Yóuzhèng Biānmǎ：455379). Liánxì Diànhuà：21416784. Diànzǐ Yóuxiāng：ioqch@tcwinvqf.cn

Chao Han Long, Room# 498, Floor# 37, He Ling Apartment, 694 Zhe Ling Road, Xingye County, Yulin, Guangxi Autonomous Region. Postal Code: 455379. Phone Number：21416784. E-mail：ioqch@tcwinvqf.cn

956。姓名: 仲孙石沛

住址（湖泊）：广西壮族自治区玉林市陆川县盛科路 920 号克咚湖（邮政编码：678900）。联系电话：85646171。电子邮箱：bjgau@ytbqmkcr.lakes.cn

Zhù zhǐ: Zhòngsūn Dàn Pèi Guǎngxī Zhuàngzú Zìzhìqū Yùlín Shì Lù Chuān Xiàn Chéng Kē Lù 920 Hào Kè Dōng Hú (Yóuzhèng Biānmǎ：678900). Liánxì Diànhuà：85646171. Diànzǐ Yóuxiāng：bjgau@ytbqmkcr.lakes.cn

Dan Pei Zhongsun, Ke Dong Lake, 920 Cheng Ke Road, Luchuan County, Yulin, Guangxi Autonomous Region. Postal Code: 678900. Phone Number：85646171. E-mail：bjgau@ytbqmkcr.lakes.cn

957。姓名: 俖化冠

住址（公司）：广西壮族自治区河池市宜州区风铁路 939 号可振有限公司（邮政编码：583407）。联系电话：17910816。电子邮箱：mctxn@sbifwqvu.biz.cn

Zhù zhǐ: Nài Huà Guān Guǎngxī Zhuàngzú Zìzhìqū Héchí Shì Yí zhōu qū Fēng Fū Lù 939 Hào Kě Zhèn Yǒuxiàn Gōngsī（Yóuzhèng Biānmǎ：583407). Liánxì Diànhuà: 17910816. Diànzǐ Yóuxiāng：mctxn@sbifwqvu.biz.cn

Hua Guan Nai, Ke Zhen Corporation, 939 Feng Fu Road, Yizhou District, Hechi, Guangxi Autonomous Region. Postal Code: 583407. Phone Number：17910816. E-mail：mctxn@sbifwqvu.biz.cn

958。姓名: 敖领龙

住址（广场）：广西壮族自治区北海市合浦县绅维路 839 号全敬广场（邮政编码：466769）。联系电话：96971187。电子邮箱：bohgk@qfrhoslp.squares.cn

Zhù zhǐ: Áo Lǐng Lóng Guǎngxī Zhuàngzú Zìzhìqū Běihǎi Shì Hépǔ Xiàn Shēn Wéi Lù 839 Hào Quán Jìng Guǎng Chǎng（Yóuzhèng Biānmǎ：466769). Liánxì Diànhuà: 96971187. Diànzǐ Yóuxiāng：bohgk@qfrhoslp.squares.cn

Ling Long Ao, Quan Jing Square, 839 Shen Wei Road, Hepu County, Beihai, Guangxi Autonomous Region. Postal Code: 466769. Phone Number：96971187. E-mail：bohgk@qfrhoslp.squares.cn

959。姓名: 熊屹院

住址（火车站）：广西壮族自治区桂林市秀峰区维自路 339 号桂林站（邮政编码：434007）。联系电话：56123127。电子邮箱：hosnk@fpishmda.chr.cn

Zhù zhǐ: Xióng Yì Yuàn Guǎngxī Zhuàngzú Zìzhìqū Guìlín Shì Xiùfēng Qū Wéi Zì Lù 339 Hào Gulín Zhàn (Yóuzhèng Biānmǎ: 434007). Liánxì Diànhuà: 56123127. Diànzǐ Yóuxiāng: hosnk@fpishmda.chr.cn

Yi Yuan Xiong, Guilin Railway Station, 339 Wei Zi Road, Xiufeng District, Guilin, Guangxi Autonomous Region. Postal Code: 434007. Phone Number: 56123127. E-mail: hosnk@fpishmda.chr.cn

960。姓名: 东易坚

住址（酒店）：广西壮族自治区防城港市上思县可盛路 622 号晖翰酒店（邮政编码：204259）。联系电话：63601114。电子邮箱：yrpgq@sbfzkaot.biz.cn

Zhù zhǐ: Dōng Yì Jiān Guǎngxī Zhuàngzú Zìzhìqū Fángchénggǎng Shì Shàng Sī Xiàn Kě Chéng Lù 622 Hào Huī Hàn Jiǔ Diàn (Yóuzhèng Biānmǎ: 204259). Liánxì Diànhuà: 63601114. Diànzǐ Yóuxiāng: yrpgq@sbfzkaot.biz.cn

Yi Jian Dong, Hui Han Hotel, 622 Ke Cheng Road, Shangsi County, Fangchenggang, Guangxi Autonomous Region. Postal Code: 204259. Phone Number: 63601114. E-mail: yrpgq@sbfzkaot.biz.cn

CHAPTER 3: NAME, SURNAME & ADDRESSES (61-90)

961。姓名: 金茂郁

住址（火车站）：广西壮族自治区河池市东兰县福浩路 130 号河池站（邮政编码：722587）。联系电话：20519430。电子邮箱：bkdyg@kayrxpwn.chr.cn

Zhù zhǐ: Jīn Mào Yù Guǎngxī Zhuàngzú Zìzhìqū Héchí Shì Dōng Lán Xiàn Fú Hào Lù 130 Hào Hécí Zhàn (Yóuzhèng Biānmǎ：722587). Liánxì Diànhuà：20519430. Diànzǐ Yóuxiāng：bkdyg@kayrxpwn.chr.cn

Mao Yu Jin, Hechi Railway Station, 130 Fu Hao Road, Donglan County, Hechi, Guangxi Autonomous Region. Postal Code: 722587. Phone Number：20519430. E-mail：bkdyg@kayrxpwn.chr.cn

962。姓名: 宗谢渊

住址（酒店）：广西壮族自治区桂林市叠彩区来全路 642 号淹浩酒店（邮政编码：526758）。联系电话：83926608。电子邮箱：adgsw@dsqvzwhr.biz.cn

Zhù zhǐ: Zōng Xiè Yuān Guǎngxī Zhuàngzú Zìzhìqū Guìlín Shì Dié Cǎi Qū Lái Quán Lù 642 Hào Yān Hào Jiǔ Diàn (Yóuzhèng Biānmǎ：526758). Liánxì Diànhuà：83926608. Diànzǐ Yóuxiāng：adgsw@dsqvzwhr.biz.cn

Xie Yuan Zong, Yan Hao Hotel, 642 Lai Quan Road, Folding Area, Guilin, Guangxi Autonomous Region. Postal Code: 526758. Phone Number：83926608. E-mail：adgsw@dsqvzwhr.biz.cn

963。姓名: 荣维禹

住址（火车站）：广西壮族自治区贵港市覃塘区冠可路 865 号贵港站（邮政编码：789451）。联系电话：58737155。电子邮箱：agrcd@wkeuxtds.chr.cn

Zhù zhǐ: Róng Wéi Yǔ Guǎngxī Zhuàngzú Zìzhìqū Guìgǎng Shì Tán Táng Qū Guàn Kě Lù 865 Hào Gugǎng Zhàn (Yóuzhèng Biānmǎ：789451). Liánxì Diànhuà：58737155. Diànzǐ Yóuxiāng：agrcd@wkeuxtds.chr.cn

Wei Yu Rong, Guigang Railway Station, 865 Guan Ke Road, Qintang District, Guigang, Guangxi Autonomous Region. Postal Code: 789451. Phone Number：58737155. E-mail：agrcd@wkeuxtds.chr.cn

964。姓名: 东方钊洵

住址（广场）：广西壮族自治区河池市天峨县铁威路 640 号翼翰广场（邮政编码：817851）。联系电话：48039978。电子邮箱：ipcbs@ecjufpry.squares.cn

Zhù zhǐ: Dōngfāng Zhāo Xún Guǎngxī Zhuàngzú Zìzhìqū Héchí Shì Tiān É Xiàn Fū Wēi Lù 640 Hào Yì Hàn Guǎng Chǎng (Yóuzhèng Biānmǎ：817851). Liánxì Diànhuà：48039978. Diànzǐ Yóuxiāng：ipcbs@ecjufpry.squares.cn

Zhao Xun Dongfang, Yi Han Square, 640 Fu Wei Road, Tiane County, Hechi, Guangxi Autonomous Region. Postal Code: 817851. Phone Number：48039978. E-mail：ipcbs@ecjufpry.squares.cn

965。姓名: 孔仲先

住址（医院）：广西壮族自治区桂林市恭城瑶族自治县威冕路 840 号友兵医院（邮政编码：524426）。联系电话：27463290。电子邮箱：fqidx@puswnbyg.health.cn

Zhù zhǐ: Kǒng Zhòng Xiān Guǎngxī Zhuàngzú Zìzhìqū Guìlín Shì Gōng Chéng Yáozú Zìzhìxiàn Wēi Miǎn Lù 840 Hào Yǒu Bīng Yī Yuàn (Yóuzhèng Biānmǎ：524426). Liánxì Diànhuà：27463290. Diànzǐ Yóuxiāng：fqidx@puswnbyg.health.cn

Zhong Xian Kong, You Bing Hospital, 840 Wei Mian Road, Gongcheng Yao Autonomous County, Guilin, Guangxi Autonomous Region. Postal Code: 524426. Phone Number：27463290. E-mail：fqidx@puswnbyg.health.cn

966。姓名: 蒯尚鸣

住址（湖泊）：广西壮族自治区柳州市城中区队食路 819 号山独湖（邮政编码：676171）。联系电话：39955063。电子邮箱：qjubz@izgvlwat.lakes.cn

Zhù zhǐ: Kuǎi Shàng Míng Guǎngxī Zhuàngzú Zìzhìqū Liǔzhōu Shì Chéngzhōng Qū Duì Yì Lù 819 Hào Shān Dú Hú (Yóuzhèng Biānmǎ：676171). Liánxì Diànhuà：39955063. Diànzǐ Yóuxiāng：qjubz@izgvlwat.lakes.cn

Shang Ming Kuai, Shan Du Lake, 819 Dui Yi Road, Chengzhong District, Liuzhou, Guangxi Autonomous Region. Postal Code: 676171. Phone Number：39955063. E-mail：qjubz@izgvlwat.lakes.cn

967。姓名: 哈立振

住址（湖泊）：广西壮族自治区防城港市港口区先王路 628 号跃威湖（邮政编码：491918）。联系电话：81401140。电子邮箱：wyomn@vazicnqb.lakes.cn

Zhù zhǐ: Hǎ Lì Zhèn Guǎngxī Zhuàngzú Zìzhìqū Fángchénggǎng Shì Gǎngkǒu Qū Xiān Wáng Lù 628 Hào Yuè Wēi Hú (Yóuzhèng Biānmǎ：491918). Liánxì Diànhuà：81401140. Diànzǐ Yóuxiāng：wyomn@vazicnqb.lakes.cn

Li Zhen Ha, Yue Wei Lake, 628 Xian Wang Road, Port Area, Fangchenggang, Guangxi Autonomous Region. Postal Code: 491918. Phone Number：81401140. E-mail：wyomn@vazicnqb.lakes.cn

968。姓名: 俚来民

住址（酒店）：广西壮族自治区崇左市凭祥市光独路 185 号南土酒店（邮政编码：803861）。联系电话：62570742。电子邮箱：hxcds@ykthaqps.biz.cn

Zhù zhǐ: Nài Lái Mín Guǎngxī Zhuàngzú Zìzhìqū Chóng Zuǒ Shì Píng xiáng shì Guāng Dú Lù 185 Hào Nán Tǔ Jiǔ Diàn (Yóuzhèng Biānmǎ：803861). Liánxì Diànhuà：62570742. Diànzǐ Yóuxiāng：hxcds@ykthaqps.biz.cn

Lai Min Nai, Nan Tu Hotel, 185 Guang Du Road, Pingxiang City, Chongzuo, Guangxi Autonomous Region. Postal Code: 803861. Phone Number：62570742. E-mail：hxcds@ykthaqps.biz.cn

969。姓名: 申钢郁

住址（广场）：广西壮族自治区玉林市陆川县舟译路 420 号金乙广场（邮政编码：678599）。联系电话：35724829。电子邮箱：cwlmv@rniewdbq.squares.cn

Zhù zhǐ: Shēn Gāng Yù Guǎngxī Zhuàngzú Zìzhìqū Yùlín Shì Lù Chuān Xiàn Zhōu Yì Lù 420 Hào Jīn Yǐ Guǎng Chǎng（Yóuzhèng Biānmǎ：678599). Liánxì Diànhuà：35724829. Diànzǐ Yóuxiāng：cwlmv@rniewdbq.squares.cn

Gang Yu Shen, Jin Yi Square, 420 Zhou Yi Road, Luchuan County, Yulin, Guangxi Autonomous Region. Postal Code: 678599. Phone Number：35724829. E-mail：cwlmv@rniewdbq.squares.cn

970。姓名: 孟学迅

住址（公共汽车站）：广西壮族自治区贺州市昭平县计磊路 241 号大队站（邮政编码：441680）。联系电话：43689171。电子邮箱：cdwoj@mfjwkzib.transport.cn

Zhù zhǐ: Mèng Xué Xùn Guǎngxī Zhuàngzú Zìzhìqū Hèzhōu Shì Zhāopíng Xiàn Jì Lěi Lù 241 Hào Dà Duì Zhàn（Yóuzhèng Biānmǎ：441680). Liánxì Diànhuà：43689171. Diànzǐ Yóuxiāng：cdwoj@mfjwkzib.transport.cn

Xue Xun Meng, Da Dui Bus Station, 241 Ji Lei Road, Zhaoping County, Hezhou, Guangxi Autonomous Region. Postal Code: 441680. Phone Number：43689171. E-mail：cdwoj@mfjwkzib.transport.cn

971。姓名: 房岐亚

住址（家庭）：广西壮族自治区桂林市雁山区先洵路 101 号谢轶公寓 47 层 347 室（邮政编码：993822）。联系电话：12363577。电子邮箱：qnrgb@zivcptne.cn

Zhù zhǐ: Fáng Qí Yà Guǎngxī Zhuàngzú Zìzhìqū Guìlín Shì Yàn Shānqū Xiān Xún Lù 101 Hào Xiè Yì Gōng Yù 47 Céng 347 Shì（Yóuzhèng Biānmǎ：993822). Liánxì Diànhuà：12363577. Diànzǐ Yóuxiāng：qnrgb@zivcptne.cn

Qi Ya Fang, Room# 347, Floor# 47, Xie Yi Apartment, 101 Xian Xun Road, Yanshan District, Guilin, Guangxi Autonomous Region. Postal Code: 993822. Phone Number：12363577. E-mail：qnrgb@zivcptne.cn

972。姓名: 通锤学

住址（家庭）：广西壮族自治区崇左市宁明县员世路 816 号洵冕公寓 43 层 485 室（邮政编码：930503）。联系电话：26032639。电子邮箱：vtgid@zpwibean.cn

Zhù zhǐ: Tōng Chuí Xué Guǎngxī Zhuàngzú Zìzhìqū Chóng Zuǒ Shì Níng Míng Xiàn Yuán Shì Lù 816 Hào Xún Miǎn Gōng Yù 43 Céng 485 Shì (Yóuzhèng Biānmǎ：930503). Liánxì Diànhuà：26032639. Diànzǐ Yóuxiāng：vtgid@zpwibean.cn

Chui Xue Tong, Room# 485, Floor# 43, Xun Mian Apartment, 816 Yuan Shi Road, Ningming County, Chongzuo, Guangxi Autonomous Region. Postal Code: 930503. Phone Number：26032639. E-mail：vtgid@zpwibean.cn

973。姓名: 狄世发

住址（机场）：广西壮族自治区河池市巴马瑶族自治县柱威路 271 号河池锡宽国际机场（邮政编码：806404）。联系电话：31454993。电子邮箱：qjdtr@njahxpld.airports.cn

Zhù zhǐ: Dí Shì Fā Guǎngxī Zhuàngzú Zìzhìqū Héchí Shì Bā Mǎ Yáozú Zìzhìxiàn Zhù Wēi Lù 271 Hào Hécí Xī Kuān Guó Jì Jī Chǎng (Yóuzhèng Biānmǎ：806404). Liánxì Diànhuà：31454993. Diànzǐ Yóuxiāng：qjdtr@njahxpld.airports.cn

Shi Fa Di, Hechi Xi Kuan International Airport, 271 Zhu Wei Road, Bama Yao Autonomous County, Hechi, Guangxi Autonomous Region. Postal Code: 806404. Phone Number：31454993. E-mail：qjdtr@njahxpld.airports.cn

974。姓名: 衡来冠

住址（机场）：广西壮族自治区贵港市港南区谢化路 274 号贵港大彬国际机场（邮政编码：394050）。联系电话：87849822。电子邮箱：dgjaw@tafocusm.airports.cn

Zhù zhǐ: Héng Lái Guān Guǎngxī Zhuàngzú Zìzhìqū Guìgǎng Shì Gǎngnán Qū Xiè Huà Lù 274 Hào Gugǎng Dài Bīn Guó Jì Jī Chǎng（Yóuzhèng Biānmǎ：394050). Liánxì Diànhuà：87849822. Diànzǐ Yóuxiāng：dgjaw@tafocusm.airports.cn

Lai Guan Heng, Guigang Dai Bin International Airport, 274 Xie Hua Road, Konan District, Guigang, Guangxi Autonomous Region. Postal Code: 394050. Phone Number：87849822. E-mail：dgjaw@tafocusm.airports.cn

975。姓名: 方陆乐

住址（火车站）：广西壮族自治区防城港市东兴市奎际路 814 号防城港站（邮政编码：776667）。联系电话：22660774。电子邮箱：iqvlc@pezcfnqb.chr.cn

Zhù zhǐ: Fāng Liù Lè Guǎngxī Zhuàngzú Zìzhìqū Fángchénggǎng Shì Dōng Xīng Shì Kuí Jì Lù 814 Hào Fángcénggǎng Zhàn（Yóuzhèng Biānmǎ：776667). Liánxì Diànhuà：22660774. Diànzǐ Yóuxiāng：iqvlc@pezcfnqb.chr.cn

Liu Le Fang, Fangchenggang Railway Station, 814 Kui Ji Road, Dongxing City, Fangchenggang, Guangxi Autonomous Region. Postal Code: 776667. Phone Number：22660774. E-mail：iqvlc@pezcfnqb.chr.cn

976。姓名: 山禹洵

住址（公园）：广西壮族自治区来宾市合山市跃石路 250 号其白公园（邮政编码：920157）。联系电话：75575141。电子邮箱：cyavg@hkrxfscm.parks.cn

Zhù zhǐ: Shān Yǔ Xún Guǎngxī Zhuàngzú Zìzhìqū Láibīn Shì Hé Shān Shì Yuè Shí Lù 250 Hào Qí Bái Gōng Yuán（Yóuzhèng Biānmǎ：920157). Liánxì Diànhuà：75575141. Diànzǐ Yóuxiāng：cyavg@hkrxfscm.parks.cn

Yu Xun Shan, Qi Bai Park, 250 Yue Shi Road, Heshan City, Laibin, Guangxi Autonomous Region. Postal Code: 920157. Phone Number：75575141. E-mail：cyavg@hkrxfscm.parks.cn

977。姓名: 寇际独

住址（公园）：广西壮族自治区崇左市凭祥市祥铭路 328 号强迅公园（邮政编码：170956）。联系电话：97912809。电子邮箱：imrjy@tqljyvie.parks.cn

Zhù zhǐ: Kòu Jì Dú Guǎngxī Zhuàngzú Zìzhìqū Chóng Zuǒ Shì Píng xiáng shì Xiáng Míng Lù 328 Hào Qiáng Xùn Gōng Yuán (Yóuzhèng Biānmǎ：170956). Liánxì Diànhuà：97912809. Diànzǐ Yóuxiāng：imrjy@tqljyvie.parks.cn

Ji Du Kou, Qiang Xun Park, 328 Xiang Ming Road, Pingxiang City, Chongzuo, Guangxi Autonomous Region. Postal Code: 170956. Phone Number：97912809. E-mail：imrjy@tqljyvie.parks.cn

978。姓名: 符珏豹

住址（公共汽车站）：广西壮族自治区钦州市钦南区独葆路 537 号茂顺站（邮政编码：736663）。联系电话：11720119。电子邮箱：qpjiy@yjcamvbe.transport.cn

Zhù zhǐ: Fú Jué Bào Guǎngxī Zhuàngzú Zìzhìqū Qīnzhōu Shì Qīn Nán Qū Dú Bǎo Lù 537 Hào Mào Shùn Zhàn (Yóuzhèng Biānmǎ：736663). Liánxì Diànhuà：11720119. Diànzǐ Yóuxiāng：qpjiy@yjcamvbe.transport.cn

Jue Bao Fu, Mao Shun Bus Station, 537 Du Bao Road, Chennan District, Qinzhou, Guangxi Autonomous Region. Postal Code: 736663. Phone Number：11720119. E-mail：qpjiy@yjcamvbe.transport.cn

979。姓名: 靳继渊

住址（博物院）：广西壮族自治区梧州市万秀区淹食路 338 号梧州博物馆（邮政编码：998340）。联系电话：47166378。电子邮箱：uvohf@dcgrwplt.museums.cn

Zhù zhǐ: Jìn Jì Yuān Guǎngxī Zhuàngzú Zìzhìqū Wúzhōu Shì Wàn Xiù Qū Yān Shí Lù 338 Hào Wúzōu Bó Wù Guǎn（Yóuzhèng Biānmǎ：998340）. Liánxì Diànhuà：47166378. Diànzǐ Yóuxiāng：uvohf@dcgrwplt.museums.cn

Ji Yuan Jin, Wuzhou Museum, 338 Yan Shi Road, Wanxiu District, Wuzhou, Guangxi Autonomous Region. Postal Code: 998340. Phone Number：47166378. E-mail：uvohf@dcgrwplt.museums.cn

980。姓名: 易大超

住址（火车站）：广西壮族自治区钦州市钦北区居星路 738 号钦州站（邮政编码：548151）。联系电话：93449146。电子邮箱：dazsx@lwesyjmv.chr.cn

Zhù zhǐ: Yì Dài Chāo Guǎngxī Zhuàngzú Zìzhìqū Qīnzhōu Shì Qīn Běi Qū Jū Xīng Lù 738 Hào Qīnzōu Zhàn（Yóuzhèng Biānmǎ：548151）. Liánxì Diànhuà：93449146. Diànzǐ Yóuxiāng：dazsx@lwesyjmv.chr.cn

Dai Chao Yi, Qinzhou Railway Station, 738 Ju Xing Road, Qinbei District, Qinzhou, Guangxi Autonomous Region. Postal Code: 548151. Phone Number：93449146. E-mail：dazsx@lwesyjmv.chr.cn

981。姓名: 壤驷近隆

住址（机场）：广西壮族自治区梧州市蒙山县启仲路 550 号梧州轶毅国际机场（邮政编码：202982）。联系电话：94167850。电子邮箱：xzmfe@otbpxjvl.airports.cn

Zhù zhǐ: Rǎngsì Jìn Lóng Guǎngxī Zhuàngzú Zìzhìqū Wúzhōu Shì Méng Shānxiàn Qǐ Zhòng Lù 550 Hào Wúzōu Yì Yì Guó Jì Jī Chǎng（Yóuzhèng Biānmǎ：202982）. Liánxì Diànhuà：94167850. Diànzǐ Yóuxiāng：xzmfe@otbpxjvl.airports.cn

Jin Long Rangsi, Wuzhou Yi Yi International Airport, 550 Qi Zhong Road, Mengshan County, Wuzhou, Guangxi Autonomous Region. Postal Code: 202982. Phone Number：94167850. E-mail：xzmfe@otbpxjvl.airports.cn

982。姓名: 晏王盛

住址（寺庙）：广西壮族自治区贺州市八步区土柱路 969 号顺人寺（邮政编码：736700）。联系电话：27338756。电子邮箱：znxdl@ryatzhjd.god.cn

Zhù zhǐ: Yàn Wáng Shèng Guǎngxī Zhuàngzú Zìzhìqū Hèzhōu Shì Bā Bù Qū Tǔ Zhù Lù 969 Hào Shùn Rén Sì (Yóuzhèng Biānmǎ：736700). Liánxì Diànhuà：27338756. Diànzǐ Yóuxiāng：znxdl@ryatzhjd.god.cn

Wang Sheng Yan, Shun Ren Temple, 969 Tu Zhu Road, Babu District, Hezhou, Guangxi Autonomous Region. Postal Code: 736700. Phone Number：27338756. E-mail：znxdl@ryatzhjd.god.cn

983。姓名: 霍克黎

住址（机场）：广西壮族自治区防城港市东兴市珂维路 644 号防城港化翰国际机场（邮政编码：930741）。联系电话：95209560。电子邮箱：qnvut@nogtlpzb.airports.cn

Zhù zhǐ: Huò Kè Lí Guǎngxī Zhuàngzú Zìzhìqū Fángchénggǎng Shì Dōng Xīng Shì Kē Wéi Lù 644 Hào Fángcénggǎng Huà Hàn Guó Jì Jī Chǎng (Yóuzhèng Biānmǎ：930741). Liánxì Diànhuà：95209560. Diànzǐ Yóuxiāng：qnvut@nogtlpzb.airports.cn

Ke Li Huo, Fangchenggang Hua Han International Airport, 644 Ke Wei Road, Dongxing City, Fangchenggang, Guangxi Autonomous Region. Postal Code: 930741. Phone Number：95209560. E-mail：qnvut@nogtlpzb.airports.cn

984。姓名: 滕化坡

住址（家庭）：广西壮族自治区北海市合浦县豹禹路 702 号澜院公寓 25 层 371 室（邮政编码：143067）。联系电话：22926585。电子邮箱：srpho@zrmfclaj.cn

Zhù zhǐ: Téng Huā Pō Guǎngxī Zhuàngzú Zìzhìqū Běihǎi Shì Hépǔ Xiàn Bào Yǔ Lù 702 Hào Lán Yuàn Gōng Yù 25 Céng 371 Shì (Yóuzhèng Biānmǎ：143067). Liánxì Diànhuà：22926585. Diànzǐ Yóuxiāng：srpho@zrmfclaj.cn

Hua Po Teng, Room# 371, Floor# 25, Lan Yuan Apartment, 702 Bao Yu Road, Hepu County, Beihai, Guangxi Autonomous Region. Postal Code: 143067. Phone Number：22926585. E-mail：srpho@zrmfclaj.cn

985。姓名: 饶冠顺

住址（公共汽车站）：广西壮族自治区梧州市蒙山县豪民路 851 号豪禹站（邮政编码：585889）。联系电话：25620062。电子邮箱：xpscw@dxvabqeo.transport.cn

Zhù zhǐ: Ráo Guàn Shùn Guǎngxī Zhuàngzú Zìzhìqū Wúzhōu Shì Méng Shānxiàn Háo Mín Lù 851 Hào Háo Yǔ Zhàn（Yóuzhèng Biānmǎ：585889). Liánxì Diànhuà：25620062. Diànzǐ Yóuxiāng：xpscw@dxvabqeo.transport.cn

Guan Shun Rao, Hao Yu Bus Station, 851 Hao Min Road, Mengshan County, Wuzhou, Guangxi Autonomous Region. Postal Code: 585889. Phone Number：25620062. E-mail：xpscw@dxvabqeo.transport.cn

986。姓名: 海桥德

住址（公园）：广西壮族自治区贵港市平南县毅隆路 729 号茂来公园（邮政编码：446652）。联系电话：76417747。电子邮箱：ecqxg@dtqaghrf.parks.cn

Zhù zhǐ: Hǎi Qiáo Dé Guǎngxī Zhuàngzú Zìzhìqū Guìgǎng Shì Píng Nán Xiàn Yì Lóng Lù 729 Hào Mào Lái Gōng Yuán（Yóuzhèng Biānmǎ：446652). Liánxì Diànhuà：76417747. Diànzǐ Yóuxiāng：ecqxg@dtqaghrf.parks.cn

Qiao De Hai, Mao Lai Park, 729 Yi Long Road, Pingnan County, Guigang, Guangxi Autonomous Region. Postal Code: 446652. Phone Number：76417747. E-mail：ecqxg@dtqaghrf.parks.cn

987。姓名: 商胜珂

住址（公园）：广西壮族自治区崇左市天等县奎食路 111 号科鸣公园（邮政编码：545973）。联系电话：12096515。电子邮箱：nhzvg@cxfbedjq.parks.cn

Zhù zhǐ: Shāng Shēng Kē Guǎngxī Zhuàngzú Zìzhìqū Chóng Zuǒ Shì Tiān Děng Xiàn Kuí Shí Lù 111 Hào Kē Míng Gōng Yuán（Yóuzhèng Biānmǎ：545973). Liánxì Diànhuà：12096515. Diànzǐ Yóuxiāng：nhzvg@cxfbedjq.parks.cn

Sheng Ke Shang, Ke Ming Park, 111 Kui Shi Road, Tiandeng County, Chongzuo, Guangxi Autonomous Region. Postal Code: 545973. Phone Number：12096515. E-mail：nhzvg@cxfbedjq.parks.cn

988。姓名：陆白大

住址（大学）：广西壮族自治区百色市田林县山冠大学食土路 608 号（邮政编码：994109）。联系电话：44288054。电子邮箱：yftzu@ophecabk.edu.cn

Zhù zhǐ: Lù Bái Dài Guǎngxī Zhuàngzú Zìzhìqū Bǎisè Shì Tiánlín Xiàn Shān Guàn DàxuéSì Tǔ Lù 608 Hào（Yóuzhèng Biānmǎ：994109). Liánxì Diànhuà：44288054. Diànzǐ Yóuxiāng：yftzu@ophecabk.edu.cn

Bai Dai Lu, Shan Guan University, 608 Si Tu Road, Tianlin County, Baise, Guangxi Autonomous Region. Postal Code: 994109. Phone Number：44288054. E-mail：yftzu@ophecabk.edu.cn

989。姓名：松乙石

住址（医院）：广西壮族自治区贵港市桂平市泽尚路 503 号兆奎医院（邮政编码：907109）。联系电话：51225798。电子邮箱：fucix@rslvybjz.health.cn

Zhù zhǐ: Sōng Yǐ Dàn Guǎngxī Zhuàngzú Zìzhìqū Guìgǎng Shì Guìpíngshì Zé Shàng Lù 503 Hào Zhào Kuí Yī Yuàn（Yóuzhèng Biānmǎ：907109). Liánxì Diànhuà：51225798. Diànzǐ Yóuxiāng：fucix@rslvybjz.health.cn

Yi Dan Song, Zhao Kui Hospital, 503 Ze Shang Road, Guiping, Guigang, Guangxi Autonomous Region. Postal Code: 907109. Phone Number：51225798. E-mail：fucix@rslvybjz.health.cn

990。姓名: 濮友继

住址（大学）：广西壮族自治区来宾市忻城县启歧大学舟汉路 575 号（邮政编码：619961）。联系电话：26646163。电子邮箱：nlfpq@uqocbela.edu.cn

Zhù zhǐ: Pú Yǒu Jì Guǎngxī Zhuàngzú Zìzhìqū Láibīn Shì Xīn Chéng Xiàn Qǐ Qí DàxuéZhōu Hàn Lù 575 Hào (Yóuzhèng Biānmǎ：619961). Liánxì Diànhuà：26646163. Diànzǐ Yóuxiāng：nlfpq@uqocbela.edu.cn

You Ji Pu, Qi Qi University, 575 Zhou Han Road, Xincheng County, Laibin, Guangxi Autonomous Region. Postal Code: 619961. Phone Number：26646163. E-mail：nlfpq@uqocbela.edu.cn

CHAPTER 4: NAME, SURNAME & ADDRESSES (91-120)

991。姓名: 郑茂科

住址（医院）：广西壮族自治区贺州市昭平县宝阳路 102 号鹤恩医院（邮政编码：382500）。联系电话：59082730。电子邮箱：libxv@bspeygjx.health.cn

Zhù zhǐ: Zhèng Mào Kē Guǎngxī Zhuàngzú Zìzhìqū Hèzhōu Shì Zhāopíng Xiàn Bǎo Yáng Lù 102 Hào Hè Ēn Yī Yuàn （Yóuzhèng Biānmǎ：382500). Liánxì Diànhuà：59082730. Diànzǐ Yóuxiāng：libxv@bspeygjx.health.cn

Mao Ke Zheng, He En Hospital, 102 Bao Yang Road, Zhaoping County, Hezhou, Guangxi Autonomous Region. Postal Code: 382500. Phone Number：59082730. E-mail：libxv@bspeygjx.health.cn

992。姓名: 汤轼涛

住址（博物院）：广西壮族自治区贵港市桂平市斌渊路 949 号贵港博物馆（邮政编码：685943）。联系电话：45379326。电子邮箱：gvwbp@wjvxniua.museums.cn

Zhù zhǐ: Tāng Shì Tāo Guǎngxī Zhuàngzú Zìzhìqū Guìgǎng Shì Guìpíngshì Bīn Yuān Lù 949 Hào Gugǎng Bó Wù Guǎn （Yóuzhèng Biānmǎ：685943). Liánxì Diànhuà：45379326. Diànzǐ Yóuxiāng：gvwbp@wjvxniua.museums.cn

Shi Tao Tang, Guigang Museum, 949 Bin Yuan Road, Guiping, Guigang, Guangxi Autonomous Region. Postal Code: 685943. Phone Number：45379326. E-mail：gvwbp@wjvxniua.museums.cn

993。姓名: 弓源焯

住址（机场）：广西壮族自治区柳州市柳江区仓学路 168 号柳州舟淹国际机场（邮政编码：635940）。联系电话：98876804。电子邮箱：qejun@nyodlxuf.airports.cn

Zhù zhǐ: Gōng Yuán Chāo Guǎngxī Zhuàngzú Zìzhìqū Liǔzhōu Shì Liǔjiāng Qū Cāng Xué Lù 168 Hào Liǔzōu Zhōu Yān Guó Jì Jī Chǎng (Yóuzhèng Biānmǎ：635940). Liánxì Diànhuà：98876804. Diànzǐ Yóuxiāng：qejun@nyodlxuf.airports.cn

Yuan Chao Gong, Liuzhou Zhou Yan International Airport, 168 Cang Xue Road, Liujiang District, Liuzhou, Guangxi Autonomous Region. Postal Code: 635940. Phone Number：98876804. E-mail：qejun@nyodlxuf.airports.cn

994。姓名: 奚葆舟

住址（酒店）：广西壮族自治区贺州市富川瑶族自治县启己路 756 号自不酒店（邮政编码：755841）。联系电话：90682789。电子邮箱：cgelt@jwruygaz.biz.cn

Zhù zhǐ: Xī Bǎo Zhōu Guǎngxī Zhuàngzú Zìzhìqū Hèzhōu Shì Fùchuān Yáozú Zìzhìxiàn Qǐ Jǐ Lù 756 Hào Zì Bù Jiǔ Diàn (Yóuzhèng Biānmǎ：755841). Liánxì Diànhuà：90682789. Diànzǐ Yóuxiāng：cgelt@jwruygaz.biz.cn

Bao Zhou Xi, Zi Bu Hotel, 756 Qi Ji Road, Fuchuan Yao Autonomous County, Hezhou, Guangxi Autonomous Region. Postal Code: 755841. Phone Number：90682789. E-mail：cgelt@jwruygaz.biz.cn

995。姓名: 楚中惟

住址（博物院）：广西壮族自治区北海市海城区尚伦路 177 号北海博物馆（邮政编码：177908）。联系电话：98331411。电子邮箱：ezurb@tmepgoui.museums.cn

Zhù zhǐ: Chǔ Zhòng Wéi Guǎngxī Zhuàngzú Zìzhìqū Běihǎi Shì Hǎi Chéngqū Shàng Lún Lù 177 Hào Běiǎi Bó Wù Guǎn (Yóuzhèng Biānmǎ：177908). Liánxì Diànhuà：98331411. Diànzǐ Yóuxiāng：ezurb@tmepgoui.museums.cn

Zhong Wei Chu, Beihai Museum, 177 Shang Lun Road, Haicheng District, Beihai, Guangxi Autonomous Region. Postal Code: 177908. Phone Number：98331411. E-mail：ezurb@tmepgoui.museums.cn

996。姓名：帅可冠

住址（湖泊）：广西壮族自治区钦州市钦北区钊铁路 495 号盛智湖（邮政编码：192184）。联系电话：95551531。电子邮箱：fktow@kjzqwecs.lakes.cn

Zhù zhǐ: Shuài Kě Guān Guǎngxī Zhuàngzú Zìzhìqū Qīnzhōu Shì Qīn Běi Qū Zhāo Tiě Lù 495 Hào Shèng Zhì Hú (Yóuzhèng Biānmǎ：192184). Liánxì Diànhuà：95551531. Diànzǐ Yóuxiāng：fktow@kjzqwecs.lakes.cn

Ke Guan Shuai, Sheng Zhi Lake, 495 Zhao Tie Road, Qinbei District, Qinzhou, Guangxi Autonomous Region. Postal Code: 192184. Phone Number：95551531. E-mail：fktow@kjzqwecs.lakes.cn

997。姓名：夏勇金

住址（医院）：广西壮族自治区南宁市良庆区王钦路 281 号洵领医院（邮政编码：276843）。联系电话：75873582。电子邮箱：jbrsv@mjaifnyr.health.cn

Zhù zhǐ: Xià Yǒng Jīn Guǎngxī Zhuàngzú Zìzhìqū Nánníng Shì Liáng Qìng Qū Wàng Qīn Lù 281 Hào Xún Lǐng Yī Yuàn (Yóuzhèng Biānmǎ：276843). Liánxì Diànhuà：75873582. Diànzǐ Yóuxiāng：jbrsv@mjaifnyr.health.cn

Yong Jin Xia, Xun Ling Hospital, 281 Wang Qin Road, Liangqing District, NanNing, Guangxi Autonomous Region. Postal Code: 276843. Phone Number：75873582. E-mail：jbrsv@mjaifnyr.health.cn

998。姓名：夔辉锡

住址（大学）：广西壮族自治区梧州市龙圩区可腾大学征游路 949 号（邮政编码：298454）。联系电话：83002945。电子邮箱：faxqk@dycmbxgk.edu.cn

Zhù zhǐ: Kuí Huī Xī Guǎngxī Zhuàngzú Zìzhìqū Wúzhōu Shì Lóng Wéi Qū Kě Téng DàxuéZhēng Yóu Lù 949 Hào (Yóuzhèng Biānmǎ：298454). Liánxì Diànhuà：83002945. Diànzǐ Yóuxiāng：faxqk@dycmbxgk.edu.cn

Hui Xi Kui, Ke Teng University, 949 Zheng You Road, Longxu District, Wuzhou, Guangxi Autonomous Region. Postal Code: 298454. Phone Number：83002945. E-mail：faxqk@dycmbxgk.edu.cn

999。姓名: 荀岐星

住址（公共汽车站）：广西壮族自治区来宾市武宣县土钊路 927 号澜焯站（邮政编码：214715）。联系电话：87415944。电子邮箱：ekgbs@nscmvgjw.transport.cn

Zhù zhǐ: Xún Qí Xīng Guǎngxī Zhuàngzú Zìzhìqū Láibīn Shì Wǔxuān Xiàn Tǔ Zhāo Lù 927 Hào Lán Chāo Zhàn (Yóuzhèng Biānmǎ：214715). Liánxì Diànhuà：87415944. Diànzǐ Yóuxiāng：ekgbs@nscmvgjw.transport.cn

Qi Xing Xun, Lan Chao Bus Station, 927 Tu Zhao Road, Wuxuan County, Laibin, Guangxi Autonomous Region. Postal Code: 214715. Phone Number：87415944. E-mail：ekgbs@nscmvgjw.transport.cn

1000。姓名: 亓官陆仲

住址（湖泊）：广西壮族自治区钦州市灵山县冠嘉路 263 号沛伦湖（邮政编码：158707）。联系电话：57972888。电子邮箱：vmjrb@gsbtruye.lakes.cn

Zhù zhǐ: Qíguān Liù Zhòng Guǎngxī Zhuàngzú Zìzhìqū Qīnzhōu Shì Língshān Xiàn Guān Jiā Lù 263 Hào Pèi Lún Hú (Yóuzhèng Biānmǎ：158707). Liánxì Diànhuà：57972888. Diànzǐ Yóuxiāng：vmjrb@gsbtruye.lakes.cn

Liu Zhong Qiguan, Pei Lun Lake, 263 Guan Jia Road, Lingshan County, Qinzhou, Guangxi Autonomous Region. Postal Code: 158707. Phone Number：57972888. E-mail：vmjrb@gsbtruye.lakes.cn

1001。姓名: 李自毅

住址（广场）：广西壮族自治区南宁市良庆区奎炯路 855 号强游广场（邮政编码：873137）。联系电话：37201319。电子邮箱：rnbop@orbtwzcg.squares.cn

Zhù zhǐ: Lǐ Zì Yì Guǎngxī Zhuàngzú Zìzhìqū Nánníng Shì Liáng Qìng Qū Kuí Jiǒng Lù 855 Hào Qiǎng Yóu Guǎng Chǎng（Yóuzhèng Biānmǎ：873137). Liánxì Diànhuà：37201319. Diànzǐ Yóuxiāng：rnbop@orbtwzcg.squares.cn

Zi Yi Li, Qiang You Square, 855 Kui Jiong Road, Liangqing District, NanNing, Guangxi Autonomous Region. Postal Code: 873137. Phone Number：37201319. E-mail：rnbop@orbtwzcg.squares.cn

1002。姓名: 宗政食光

住址（家庭）：广西壮族自治区来宾市合山市发继路 571 号水坚公寓 21 层 432 室（邮政编码：242332）。联系电话：60477295。电子邮箱：vzrcy@ntlrvpab.cn

Zhù zhǐ: Zōngzhèng Sì Guāng Guǎngxī Zhuàngzú Zìzhìqū Láibīn Shì Hé Shān Shì Fā Jì Lù 571 Hào Shuǐ Jiān Gōng Yù 21 Céng 432 Shì（Yóuzhèng Biānmǎ：242332). Liánxì Diànhuà：60477295. Diànzǐ Yóuxiāng：vzrcy@ntlrvpab.cn

Si Guang Zongzheng, Room# 432, Floor# 21, Shui Jian Apartment, 571 Fa Ji Road, Heshan City, Laibin, Guangxi Autonomous Region. Postal Code: 242332. Phone Number：60477295. E-mail：vzrcy@ntlrvpab.cn

1003。姓名: 乌桥澜

住址（酒店）：广西壮族自治区柳州市柳江区译铭路 740 号威屹酒店（邮政编码：616448）。联系电话：87185277。电子邮箱：jfatq@akhndmqi.biz.cn

Zhù zhǐ: Wū Qiáo Lán Guǎngxī Zhuàngzú Zìzhìqū Liǔzhōu Shì Liǔjiāng Qū Yì Míng Lù 740 Hào Wēi Yì Jiǔ Diàn（Yóuzhèng Biānmǎ：616448). Liánxì Diànhuà：87185277. Diànzǐ Yóuxiāng：jfatq@akhndmqi.biz.cn

Qiao Lan Wu, Wei Yi Hotel, 740 Yi Ming Road, Liujiang District, Liuzhou, Guangxi Autonomous Region. Postal Code: 616448. Phone Number：87185277. E-mail：jfatq@akhndmqi.biz.cn

1004。姓名: 高智铁

住址（博物院）：广西壮族自治区南宁市横州市陆辙路 682 号南宁博物馆（邮政编码：724338）。联系电话：42821864。电子邮箱：xkqjl@jeknglzt.museums.cn

Zhù zhǐ: Gāo Zhì Fū Guǎngxī Zhuàngzú Zìzhìqū Nánníng Shì Héng Zhōu Shì Liù Zhé Lù 682 Hào Nánníng Bó Wù Guǎn (Yóuzhèng Biānmǎ：724338). Liánxì Diànhuà：42821864. Diànzǐ Yóuxiāng：xkqjl@jeknglzt.museums.cn

Zhi Fu Gao, NanNing Museum, 682 Liu Zhe Road, Hengzhou, NanNing, Guangxi Autonomous Region. Postal Code: 724338. Phone Number：42821864. E-mail：xkqjl@jeknglzt.museums.cn

1005。姓名: 蔡奎振

住址（医院）：广西壮族自治区河池市罗城仫佬族自治县队山路 333 号陶臻医院（邮政编码：665670）。联系电话：79417855。电子邮箱：sdjcb@vxyzmqjk.health.cn

Zhù zhǐ: Cài Kuí Zhèn Guǎngxī Zhuàngzú Zìzhìqū Héchí Shì Luō Chéng Mù Lǎo Zú Zìzhìxiàn Duì Shān Lù 333 Hào Táo Zhēn Yī Yuàn (Yóuzhèng Biānmǎ：665670). Liánxì Diànhuà：79417855. Diànzǐ Yóuxiāng：sdjcb@vxyzmqjk.health.cn

Kui Zhen Cai, Tao Zhen Hospital, 333 Dui Shan Road, Luocheng Mulao Autonomous County, Hechi, Guangxi Autonomous Region. Postal Code: 665670. Phone Number：79417855. E-mail：sdjcb@vxyzmqjk.health.cn

1006。姓名: 桂敬近

住址（寺庙）：广西壮族自治区河池市都安瑶族自治县隆翰路 159 号可铁寺（邮政编码：461575）。联系电话：13349300。电子邮箱：msgwi@tavkoqfl.god.cn

Zhù zhǐ: Guì Jìng Jìn Guǎngxī Zhuàngzú Zìzhìqū Héchí Shì Dū Ān Yáozú Zìzhìxiàn Lóng Hàn Lù 159 Hào Kě Fū Sì (Yóuzhèng Biānmǎ：461575). Liánxì Diànhuà：13349300. Diànzǐ Yóuxiāng：msgwi@tavkoqfl.god.cn

Jing Jin Gui, Ke Fu Temple, 159 Long Han Road, Duan Yao Autonomous County, Hechi, Guangxi Autonomous Region. Postal Code: 461575. Phone Number：13349300. E-mail：msgwi@tavkoqfl.god.cn

1007。姓名: 贲光黎

住址（酒店）：广西壮族自治区玉林市容县兵启路 320 号祥科酒店（邮政编码：791032）。联系电话：72782789。电子邮箱：tijlq@goydknpm.biz.cn

Zhù zhǐ: Bēn Guāng Lí Guǎngxī Zhuàngzú Zìzhìqū Yùlín Shì Róngxiàn Bīng Qǐ Lù 320 Hào Xiáng Kē Jiǔ Diàn （Yóuzhèng Biānmǎ：791032). Liánxì Diànhuà：72782789. Diànzǐ Yóuxiāng：tijlq@goydknpm.biz.cn

Guang Li Ben, Xiang Ke Hotel, 320 Bing Qi Road, Rong County, Yulin, Guangxi Autonomous Region. Postal Code: 791032. Phone Number：72782789. E-mail：tijlq@goydknpm.biz.cn

1008。姓名: 于陆尚

住址（公园）：广西壮族自治区百色市凌云县源庆路 497 号辙可公园（邮政编码：878830）。联系电话：39092115。电子邮箱：iyahe@nybevsfk.parks.cn

Zhù zhǐ: Yú Lù Shàng Guǎngxī Zhuàngzú Zìzhìqū Bǎisè Shì Língyún Xiàn Yuán Qìng Lù 497 Hào Zhé Kě Gōng Yuán （Yóuzhèng Biānmǎ：878830). Liánxì Diànhuà：39092115. Diànzǐ Yóuxiāng：iyahe@nybevsfk.parks.cn

Lu Shang Yu, Zhe Ke Park, 497 Yuan Qing Road, Lingyun County, Baise, Guangxi Autonomous Region. Postal Code: 878830. Phone Number：39092115. E-mail：iyahe@nybevsfk.parks.cn

1009。姓名: 池石科

住址（湖泊）：广西壮族自治区崇左市江州区学院路 909 号兆风湖（邮政编码：266346）。联系电话：42276402。电子邮箱：hsprz@csjqynzu.lakes.cn

Zhù zhǐ: Chí Dàn Kē Guǎngxī Zhuàngzú Zìzhìqū Chóng Zuǒ Shì Jiāng Zhōu Qū Xué Yuàn Lù 909 Hào Zhào Fēng Hú (Yóuzhèng Biānmǎ: 266346). Liánxì Diànhuà: 42276402. Diànzǐ Yóuxiāng: hsprz@csjqynzu.lakes.cn

Dan Ke Chi, Zhao Feng Lake, 909 Xue Yuan Road, Jiangzhou District, Chongzuo, Guangxi Autonomous Region. Postal Code: 266346. Phone Number: 42276402. E-mail: hsprz@csjqynzu.lakes.cn

1010。姓名: 司空铭涛

住址（机场）：广西壮族自治区柳州市三江侗族自治县沛仓路 957 号柳州沛俊国际机场（邮政编码：970933）。联系电话：70367016。电子邮箱：tgjve@fcuvgndb.airports.cn

Zhù zhǐ: Sīkōng Míng Tāo Guǎngxī Zhuàngzú Zìzhìqū Liǔzhōu Shì Sānjiāng Dòngzú Zìzhìxiàn Bèi Cāng Lù 957 Hào Liǔzōu Bèi Jùn Guó Jì Jī Chǎng (Yóuzhèng Biānmǎ: 970933). Liánxì Diànhuà: 70367016. Diànzǐ Yóuxiāng: tgjve@fcuvgndb.airports.cn

Ming Tao Sikong, Liuzhou Bei Jun International Airport, 957 Bei Cang Road, Sanjiang Dong Autonomous County, Liuzhou, Guangxi Autonomous Region. Postal Code: 970933. Phone Number: 70367016. E-mail: tgjve@fcuvgndb.airports.cn

1011。姓名: 卫冠顺

住址（医院）：广西壮族自治区河池市东兰县黎石路 736 号世葆医院（邮政编码：925579）。联系电话：19951392。电子邮箱：meutj@mqkgsrvd.health.cn

Zhù zhǐ: Wèi Guàn Shùn Guǎngxī Zhuàngzú Zìzhìqū Héchí Shì Dōng Lán Xiàn Lí Shí Lù 736 Hào Shì Bǎo Yī Yuàn (Yóuzhèng Biānmǎ: 925579). Liánxì Diànhuà: 19951392. Diànzǐ Yóuxiāng: meutj@mqkgsrvd.health.cn

Guan Shun Wei, Shi Bao Hospital, 736 Li Shi Road, Donglan County, Hechi, Guangxi Autonomous Region. Postal Code: 925579. Phone Number：19951392. E-mail：meutj@mqkgsrvd.health.cn

1012。姓名: 咸熔稼

住址（火车站）：广西壮族自治区梧州市藤县发全路 709 号梧州站（邮政编码：327613）。联系电话：56031276。电子邮箱：cuwxh@mcoaznil.chr.cn

Zhù zhǐ: Xián Róng Jià Guǎngxī Zhuàngzú Zìzhìqū Wúzhōu Shì Téng Xiàn Fā Quán Lù 709 Hào Wúzōu Zhàn（Yóuzhèng Biānmǎ：327613）. Liánxì Diànhuà：56031276. Diànzǐ Yóuxiāng：cuwxh@mcoaznil.chr.cn

Rong Jia Xian, Wuzhou Railway Station, 709 Fa Quan Road, Fuji County, Wuzhou, Guangxi Autonomous Region. Postal Code: 327613. Phone Number：56031276. E-mail：cuwxh@mcoaznil.chr.cn

1013。姓名: 周盛涛

住址（大学）：广西壮族自治区玉林市博白县大超大学居石路 574 号（邮政编码：121148）。联系电话：64510682。电子邮箱：idqtp@tmdrnofk.edu.cn

Zhù zhǐ: Zhōu Shèng Tāo Guǎngxī Zhuàngzú Zìzhìqū Yùlín Shì Bó Bái Xiàn Dà Chāo DàxuéJū Dàn Lù 574 Hào（Yóuzhèng Biānmǎ：121148）. Liánxì Diànhuà：64510682. Diànzǐ Yóuxiāng：idqtp@tmdrnofk.edu.cn

Sheng Tao Zhou, Da Chao University, 574 Ju Dan Road, Bobai County, Yulin, Guangxi Autonomous Region. Postal Code: 121148. Phone Number：64510682. E-mail：idqtp@tmdrnofk.edu.cn

1014。姓名: 百里兆译

住址（机场）：广西壮族自治区河池市天峨县胜洵路 861 号河池稼乙国际机场（邮政编码：817270）。联系电话：44278649。电子邮箱：kywec@mlpwtjhb.airports.cn

Zhù zhǐ: Bǎilǐ Zhào Yì Guǎngxī Zhuàngzú Zìzhìqū Héchí Shì Tiān É Xiàn Shēng Xún Lù 861 Hào Hécí Jià Yǐ Guó Jì Jī Chǎng（Yóuzhèng Biānmǎ：817270). Liánxì Diànhuà：44278649. Diànzǐ Yóuxiāng：kywec@mlpwtjhb.airports.cn

Zhao Yi Baili, Hechi Jia Yi International Airport, 861 Sheng Xun Road, Tiane County, Hechi, Guangxi Autonomous Region. Postal Code: 817270. Phone Number：44278649. E-mail：kywec@mlpwtjhb.airports.cn

1015。姓名: 华原锡

住址（公司）：广西壮族自治区柳州市柳北区兆渊路 345 号腾全有限公司（邮政编码：534270）。联系电话：80601673。电子邮箱：awfog@ydatqulm.biz.cn

Zhù zhǐ: Huà Yuán Xī Guǎngxī Zhuàngzú Zìzhìqū Liǔzhōu Shì Liǔběi Qū Zhào Yuán Lù 345 Hào Téng Quán Yǒuxiàn Gōngsī（Yóuzhèng Biānmǎ：534270). Liánxì Diànhuà：80601673. Diànzǐ Yóuxiāng：awfog@ydatqulm.biz.cn

Yuan Xi Hua, Teng Quan Corporation, 345 Zhao Yuan Road, Liubei District, Liuzhou, Guangxi Autonomous Region. Postal Code: 534270. Phone Number：80601673. E-mail：awfog@ydatqulm.biz.cn

1016。姓名: 相豹克

住址（公司）：广西壮族自治区贺州市昭平县国浩路 542 号轶葛有限公司（邮政编码：111777）。联系电话：97244706。电子邮箱：tlrnj@nkbhxgcv.biz.cn

Zhù zhǐ: Xiàng Bào Kè Guǎngxī Zhuàngzú Zìzhìqū Hèzhōu Shì Zhāopíng Xiàn Guó Hào Lù 542 Hào Yì Gé Yǒuxiàn Gōngsī（Yóuzhèng Biānmǎ：111777). Liánxì Diànhuà：97244706. Diànzǐ Yóuxiāng：tlrnj@nkbhxgcv.biz.cn

Bao Ke Xiang, Yi Ge Corporation, 542 Guo Hao Road, Zhaoping County, Hezhou, Guangxi Autonomous Region. Postal Code: 111777. Phone Number：97244706. E-mail：tlrnj@nkbhxgcv.biz.cn

1017。姓名: 纪炯己

住址（医院）：广西壮族自治区梧州市岑溪市亮成路 976 号岐冕医院（邮政编码：631215）。联系电话：50000663。电子邮箱：jzmex@cwioqexm.health.cn

Zhù zhǐ: Jì Jiǒng Jǐ Guǎngxī Zhuàngzú Zìzhìqū Wúzhōu Shì Cénxī Shì Liàng Chéng Lù 976 Hào Qí Miǎn Yī Yuàn（Yóuzhèng Biānmǎ：631215）. Liánxì Diànhuà：50000663. Diànzǐ Yóuxiāng：jzmex@cwioqexm.health.cn

Jiong Ji Ji, Qi Mian Hospital, 976 Liang Cheng Road, Cenxi City, Wuzhou, Guangxi Autonomous Region. Postal Code: 631215. Phone Number：50000663. E-mail：jzmex@cwioqexm.health.cn

1018。姓名: 田强国

住址（医院）：广西壮族自治区防城港市港口区甫近路 284 号鸣源医院（邮政编码：781775）。联系电话：21793665。电子邮箱：kaebp@roublqzs.health.cn

Zhù zhǐ: Tián Qiáng Guó Guǎngxī Zhuàngzú Zìzhìqū Fángchénggǎng Shì Gǎngkǒu Qū Fǔ Jìn Lù 284 Hào Míng Yuán Yī Yuàn（Yóuzhèng Biānmǎ：781775）. Liánxì Diànhuà：21793665. Diànzǐ Yóuxiāng：kaebp@roublqzs.health.cn

Qiang Guo Tian, Ming Yuan Hospital, 284 Fu Jin Road, Port Area, Fangchenggang, Guangxi Autonomous Region. Postal Code: 781775. Phone Number：21793665. E-mail：kaebp@roublqzs.health.cn

1019。姓名: 芮楚沛

住址（火车站）：广西壮族自治区来宾市兴宾区其恩路 167 号来宾站（邮政编码：271812）。联系电话：31333150。电子邮箱：nezos@pwjinfxz.chr.cn

Zhù zhǐ: Ruì Chǔ Bèi Guǎngxī Zhuàngzú Zìzhìqū Láibīn Shì Xìng Bīn Qū Qí Ēn Lù 167 Hào Láibīn Zhàn（Yóuzhèng Biānmǎ：271812）. Liánxì Diànhuà：31333150. Diànzǐ Yóuxiāng：nezos@pwjinfxz.chr.cn

Chu Bei Rui, Laibin Railway Station, 167 Qi En Road, Xingbin District, Laibin, Guangxi Autonomous Region. Postal Code: 271812. Phone Number：31333150. E-mail：nezos@pwjinfxz.chr.cn

1020。姓名: 母隆钊

住址（大学）：广西壮族自治区钦州市灵山县咚亚大学大可路 186 号（邮政编码：529031）。联系电话：37662931。电子邮箱：vzmgp@vikmxczo.edu.cn

Zhù zhǐ: Mǔ Lóng Zhāo Guǎngxī Zhuàngzú Zìzhìqū Qīnzhōu Shì Língshān Xiàn Dōng Yà DàxuéDài Kě Lù 186 Hào (Yóuzhèng Biānmǎ：529031). Liánxì Diànhuà：37662931. Diànzǐ Yóuxiāng：vzmgp@vikmxczo.edu.cn

Long Zhao Mu, Dong Ya University, 186 Dai Ke Road, Lingshan County, Qinzhou, Guangxi Autonomous Region. Postal Code: 529031. Phone Number：37662931. E-mail：vzmgp@vikmxczo.edu.cn

CHAPTER 5: NAME, SURNAME & ADDRESSES (121-150)

1021。姓名: 水发成

住址（广场）：广西壮族自治区贺州市钟山县龙陆路 813 号守浩广场（邮政编码：684468）。联系电话：39845304。电子邮箱：izdhk@gmwleonj.squares.cn

Zhù zhǐ: Shuǐ Fā Chéng Guǎngxī Zhuàngzú Zìzhìqū Hèzhōu Shì Zhōng Shān Xiàn Lóng Lù Lù 813 Hào Shǒu Hào Guǎng Chǎng (Yóuzhèng Biānmǎ：684468). Liánxì Diànhuà：39845304. Diànzǐ Yóuxiāng：izdhk@gmwleonj.squares.cn

Fa Cheng Shui, Shou Hao Square, 813 Long Lu Road, Zhongshan County, Hezhou, Guangxi Autonomous Region. Postal Code: 684468. Phone Number：39845304. E-mail：izdhk@gmwleonj.squares.cn

1022。姓名: 平龙泽

住址（寺庙）：广西壮族自治区崇左市大新县翼恩路 768 号惟南寺（邮政编码：654805）。联系电话：74688703。电子邮箱：fbmga@wmaxghpd.god.cn

Zhù zhǐ: Píng Lóng Zé Guǎngxī Zhuàngzú Zìzhìqū Chóng Zuǒ Shì Dà Xīn Xiàn Yì Ēn Lù 768 Hào Wéi Nán Sì (Yóuzhèng Biānmǎ：654805). Liánxì Diànhuà：74688703. Diànzǐ Yóuxiāng：fbmga@wmaxghpd.god.cn

Long Ze Ping, Wei Nan Temple, 768 Yi En Road, Daxin County, Chongzuo, Guangxi Autonomous Region. Postal Code: 654805. Phone Number：74688703. E-mail：fbmga@wmaxghpd.god.cn

1023。姓名: 侯惟大

住址（广场）：广西壮族自治区南宁市横州市焯仓路 493 号亭友广场（邮政编码：526267）。联系电话：57816277。电子邮箱：klypn@ayentbfj.squares.cn

Zhù zhǐ: Hóu Wéi Dà Guǎngxī Zhuàngzú Zìzhìqū Nánníng Shì Héng Zhōu Shì Chāo Cāng Lù 493 Hào Tíng Yǒu Guǎng Chǎng (Yóuzhèng Biānmǎ：526267). Liánxì Diànhuà：57816277. Diànzǐ Yóuxiāng：klypn@ayentbfj.squares.cn

Wei Da Hou, Ting You Square, 493 Chao Cang Road, Hengzhou, NanNing, Guangxi Autonomous Region. Postal Code: 526267. Phone Number：57816277. E-mail：klypn@ayentbfj.squares.cn

1024。姓名: 郁进沛

住址（湖泊）：广西壮族自治区河池市都安瑶族自治县葛顺路 504 号来稼湖（邮政编码：716199）。联系电话：39215945。电子邮箱：cwvem@saziuwvq.lakes.cn

Zhù zhǐ: Yù Jìn Pèi Guǎngxī Zhuàngzú Zìzhìqū Héchí Shì Dū Ān Yáozú Zìzhìxiàn Gé Shùn Lù 504 Hào Lái Jià Hú (Yóuzhèng Biānmǎ：716199). Liánxì Diànhuà：39215945. Diànzǐ Yóuxiāng：cwvem@saziuwvq.lakes.cn

Jin Pei Yu, Lai Jia Lake, 504 Ge Shun Road, Duan Yao Autonomous County, Hechi, Guangxi Autonomous Region. Postal Code: 716199. Phone Number：39215945. E-mail：cwvem@saziuwvq.lakes.cn

1025。姓名: 夏歧金

住址（广场）：广西壮族自治区百色市凌云县骥星路 657 号胜成广场（邮政编码：466270）。联系电话：95872694。电子邮箱：gkomw@tmzpubje.squares.cn

Zhù zhǐ: Xià Qí Jīn Guǎngxī Zhuàngzú Zìzhìqū Bǎisè Shì Língyún Xiàn Jì Xīng Lù 657 Hào Shēng Chéng Guǎng Chǎng (Yóuzhèng Biānmǎ：466270). Liánxì Diànhuà：95872694. Diànzǐ Yóuxiāng：gkomw@tmzpubje.squares.cn

Qi Jin Xia, Sheng Cheng Square, 657 Ji Xing Road, Lingyun County, Baise, Guangxi Autonomous Region. Postal Code: 466270. Phone Number：95872694. E-mail：gkomw@tmzpubje.squares.cn

1026。姓名: 昌可水

住址（寺庙）：广西壮族自治区百色市德保县兵游路 401 号原学寺（邮政编码：684273）。联系电话：31012938。电子邮箱：iapgw@fqwbrolc.god.cn

Zhù zhǐ: Chāng Kě Shuǐ Guǎngxī Zhuàngzú Zìzhìqū Bǎisè Shì Dé Bǎo Xiàn Bīng Yóu Lù 401 Hào Yuán Xué Sì (Yóuzhèng Biānmǎ：684273). Liánxì Diànhuà：31012938. Diànzǐ Yóuxiāng：iapgw@fqwbrolc.god.cn

Ke Shui Chang, Yuan Xue Temple, 401 Bing You Road, Debao County, Baise, Guangxi Autonomous Region. Postal Code: 684273. Phone Number：31012938. E-mail：iapgw@fqwbrolc.god.cn

1027。姓名: 万俟计斌

住址（机场）：广西壮族自治区北海市合浦县先乙路 686 号北海钢阳国际机场（邮政编码：984753）。联系电话：37135361。电子邮箱：qdcli@wkpcqufx.airports.cn

Zhù zhǐ: Mòqí Jì Bīn Guǎngxī Zhuàngzú Zìzhìqū Běihǎi Shì Hépǔ Xiàn Xiān Yǐ Lù 686 Hào Běiǎi Gāng Yáng Guó Jì Jī Chǎng (Yóuzhèng Biānmǎ：984753). Liánxì Diànhuà：37135361. Diànzǐ Yóuxiāng：qdcli@wkpcqufx.airports.cn

Ji Bin Moqi, Beihai Gang Yang International Airport, 686 Xian Yi Road, Hepu County, Beihai, Guangxi Autonomous Region. Postal Code: 984753. Phone Number：37135361. E-mail：qdcli@wkpcqufx.airports.cn

1028。姓名: 万钢祥

住址（火车站）：广西壮族自治区梧州市岑溪市可桥路 850 号梧州站（邮政编码：617108）。联系电话：48747812。电子邮箱：ndkah@lwbpdekv.chr.cn

Zhù zhǐ: Wàn Gāng Xiáng Guǎngxī Zhuàngzú Zìzhìqū Wúzhōu Shì Cénxī Shì Kě Qiáo Lù 850 Hào Wúzōu Zhàn (Yóuzhèng Biānmǎ：617108). Liánxì Diànhuà：48747812. Diànzǐ Yóuxiāng：ndkah@lwbpdekv.chr.cn

Gang Xiang Wan, Wuzhou Railway Station, 850 Ke Qiao Road, Cenxi City, Wuzhou, Guangxi Autonomous Region. Postal Code: 617108. Phone Number：48747812. E-mail：ndkah@lwbpdekv.chr.cn

1029。姓名: 毛仓珂

住址（公园）：广西壮族自治区钦州市浦北县化盛路 344 号化桥公园（邮政编码：650032）。联系电话：97687109。电子邮箱：zgjnk@zvpayfki.parks.cn

Zhù zhǐ: Máo Cāng Kē Guǎngxī Zhuàngzú Zìzhìqū Qīnzhōu Shì Pǔ Běi Xiàn Huā Shèng Lù 344 Hào Huā Qiáo Gōng Yuán（Yóuzhèng Biānmǎ：650032). Liánxì Diànhuà：97687109. Diànzǐ Yóuxiāng：zgjnk@zvpayfki.parks.cn

Cang Ke Mao, Hua Qiao Park, 344 Hua Sheng Road, Pubei County, Qinzhou, Guangxi Autonomous Region. Postal Code: 650032. Phone Number：97687109. E-mail：zgjnk@zvpayfki.parks.cn

1030。姓名: 狄愈秀

住址（家庭）：广西壮族自治区贵港市覃塘区立坡路 356 号大德公寓 48 层 340 室（邮政编码：681372）。联系电话：87164882。电子邮箱：oxmbk@xgrotehf.cn

Zhù zhǐ: Dí Yù Xiù Guǎngxī Zhuàngzú Zìzhìqū Guìgǎng Shì Tán Táng Qū Lì Pō Lù 356 Hào Dài Dé Gōng Yù 48 Céng 340 Shì（Yóuzhèng Biānmǎ：681372). Liánxì Diànhuà：87164882. Diànzǐ Yóuxiāng：oxmbk@xgrotehf.cn

Yu Xiu Di, Room# 340, Floor# 48, Dai De Apartment, 356 Li Po Road, Qintang District, Guigang, Guangxi Autonomous Region. Postal Code: 681372. Phone Number：87164882. E-mail：oxmbk@xgrotehf.cn

1031。姓名: 匡祥乙

住址（广场）：广西壮族自治区南宁市西乡塘区洵冠路 616 号威民广场（邮政编码：994307）。联系电话：15832925。电子邮箱：yoiha@rmigpvnj.squares.cn

Zhù zhǐ: Kuāng Xiáng Yǐ Guǎngxī Zhuàngzú Zìzhìqū Nánníng Shì Xī Xiāng Táng Qū Xún Guàn Lù 616 Hào Wēi Mín Guǎng Chǎng (Yóuzhèng Biānmǎ：994307). Liánxì Diànhuà：15832925. Diànzǐ Yóuxiāng：yoiha@rmigpvnj.squares.cn

Xiang Yi Kuang, Wei Min Square, 616 Xun Guan Road, Xixiangtang District, NanNing, Guangxi Autonomous Region. Postal Code: 994307. Phone Number：15832925. E-mail：yoiha@rmigpvnj.squares.cn

1032。姓名: 成禹彬

住址（酒店）：广西壮族自治区南宁市兴宁区冠振路 462 号葛迅酒店（邮政编码：625025）。联系电话：99091597。电子邮箱：awfsd@lficqzgj.biz.cn

Zhù zhǐ: Chéng Yǔ Bīn Guǎngxī Zhuàngzú Zìzhìqū Nánníng Shì Xìng Níng Qū Guàn Zhèn Lù 462 Hào Gé Xùn Jiǔ Diàn (Yóuzhèng Biānmǎ：625025). Liánxì Diànhuà：99091597. Diànzǐ Yóuxiāng：awfsd@lficqzgj.biz.cn

Yu Bin Cheng, Ge Xun Hotel, 462 Guan Zhen Road, Xingning District, NanNing, Guangxi Autonomous Region. Postal Code: 625025. Phone Number：99091597. E-mail：awfsd@lficqzgj.biz.cn

1033。姓名: 伏强白

住址（广场）：广西壮族自治区崇左市江州区克洵路 250 号甫鹤广场（邮政编码：150574）。联系电话：16581492。电子邮箱：fynkl@wsrjegta.squares.cn

Zhù zhǐ: Fú Qiǎng Bái Guǎngxī Zhuàngzú Zìzhìqū Chóng Zuǒ Shì Jiāng Zhōu Qū Kè Xún Lù 250 Hào Fǔ Hè Guǎng Chǎng (Yóuzhèng Biānmǎ：150574). Liánxì Diànhuà：16581492. Diànzǐ Yóuxiāng：fynkl@wsrjegta.squares.cn

Qiang Bai Fu, Fu He Square, 250 Ke Xun Road, Jiangzhou District, Chongzuo, Guangxi Autonomous Region. Postal Code: 150574. Phone Number：16581492. E-mail：fynkl@wsrjegta.squares.cn

1034。姓名: 莫九钊

住址（大学）：广西壮族自治区梧州市苍梧县迅岐大学进禹路 190 号（邮政编码：912150）。联系电话：90780693。电子邮箱：cnhrw@pqlcueja.edu.cn

Zhù zhǐ: Mò Jiǔ Zhāo Guǎngxī Zhuàngzú Zìzhìqū Wúzhōu Shì Cāng Wú Xiàn Xùn Qí DàxuéJìn Yǔ Lù 190 Hào（Yóuzhèng Biānmǎ：912150）. Liánxì Diànhuà：90780693. Diànzǐ Yóuxiāng：cnhrw@pqlcueja.edu.cn

Jiu Zhao Mo, Xun Qi University, 190 Jin Yu Road, Cangwu County, Wuzhou, Guangxi Autonomous Region. Postal Code: 912150. Phone Number：90780693. E-mail：cnhrw@pqlcueja.edu.cn

1035。姓名: 平祥葆

住址（博物院）：广西壮族自治区桂林市恭城瑶族自治县智陆路 921 号桂林博物馆（邮政编码：438806）。联系电话：12670906。电子邮箱：uebdh@sntwfcvz.museums.cn

Zhù zhǐ: Píng Xiáng Bǎo Guǎngxī Zhuàngzú Zìzhìqū Guìlín Shì Gōng Chéng Yáozú Zìzhìxiàn Zhì Lù Lù 921 Hào Gulín Bó Wù Guǎn（Yóuzhèng Biānmǎ：438806）. Liánxì Diànhuà：12670906. Diànzǐ Yóuxiāng：uebdh@sntwfcvz.museums.cn

Xiang Bao Ping, Guilin Museum, 921 Zhi Lu Road, Gongcheng Yao Autonomous County, Guilin, Guangxi Autonomous Region. Postal Code: 438806. Phone Number：12670906. E-mail：uebdh@sntwfcvz.museums.cn

1036。姓名: 蔺不领

住址（公共汽车站）：广西壮族自治区来宾市合山市圣学路 239 号鹤斌站（邮政编码：327293）。联系电话：26564782。电子邮箱：kpuqm@phdqubae.transport.cn

Zhù zhǐ: Lìn Bù Lǐng Guǎngxī Zhuàngzú Zìzhìqū Láibīn Shì Hé Shān Shì Shèng Xué Lù 239 Hào Hè Bīn Zhàn（Yóuzhèng Biānmǎ：327293）. Liánxì Diànhuà：26564782. Diànzǐ Yóuxiāng：kpuqm@phdqubae.transport.cn

Bu Ling Lin, He Bin Bus Station, 239 Sheng Xue Road, Heshan City, Laibin, Guangxi Autonomous Region. Postal Code: 327293. Phone Number：26564782. E-mail：kpuqm@phdqubae.transport.cn

1037。姓名: 舒臻锡

住址（机场）：广西壮族自治区梧州市苍梧县恩俊路 719 号梧州化强国际机场（邮政编码：630520）。联系电话：68436160。电子邮箱：tdnji@vnhsjcxr.airports.cn

Zhù zhǐ: Shū Zhēn Xī Guǎngxī Zhuàngzú Zìzhìqū Wúzhōu Shì Cāng Wú Xiàn Ēn Jùn Lù 719 Hào Wúzōu Huà Qiǎng Guó Jì Jī Chǎng (Yóuzhèng Biānmǎ：630520). Liánxì Diànhuà：68436160. Diànzǐ Yóuxiāng：tdnji@vnhsjcxr.airports.cn

Zhen Xi Shu, Wuzhou Hua Qiang International Airport, 719 En Jun Road, Cangwu County, Wuzhou, Guangxi Autonomous Region. Postal Code: 630520. Phone Number：68436160. E-mail：tdnji@vnhsjcxr.airports.cn

1038。姓名: 郏盛民

住址（公共汽车站）：广西壮族自治区桂林市龙胜各族自治县大秀路 659 号渊乐站（邮政编码：718562）。联系电话：46729152。电子邮箱：iwubf@fadwnpir.transport.cn

Zhù zhǐ: Jiá Chéng Mín Guǎngxī Zhuàngzú Zìzhìqū Guìlín Shì Lóng Shèng Gè Zú Zìzhìxiàn Dài Xiù Lù 659 Hào Yuān Lè Zhàn (Yóuzhèng Biānmǎ：718562). Liánxì Diànhuà：46729152. Diànzǐ Yóuxiāng：iwubf@fadwnpir.transport.cn

Cheng Min Jia, Yuan Le Bus Station, 659 Dai Xiu Road, Longsheng Autonomous County Of All Nationalities, Guilin, Guangxi Autonomous Region. Postal Code: 718562. Phone Number：46729152. E-mail：iwubf@fadwnpir.transport.cn

1039。姓名: 苗渊钢

住址（大学）：广西壮族自治区百色市平果市铭红大学山伦路 266 号（邮政编码：489516）。联系电话：22781261。电子邮箱：wflcy@yzaohlmu.edu.cn

Zhù zhǐ: Miáo Yuān Gāng Guǎngxī Zhuàngzú Zìzhìqū Bǎisè Shì Píng Guǒ Shì Míng Hóng DàxuéShān Lún Lù 266 Hào (Yóuzhèng Biānmǎ：489516). Liánxì Diànhuà：22781261. Diànzǐ Yóuxiāng：wflcy@yzaohlmu.edu.cn

Yuan Gang Miao, Ming Hong University, 266 Shan Lun Road, Pingguo City, Baise, Guangxi Autonomous Region. Postal Code: 489516. Phone Number：22781261. E-mail：wflcy@yzaohlmu.edu.cn

1040。姓名: 钟石全

住址（酒店）：广西壮族自治区桂林市阳朔县俊九路 762 号渊土酒店（邮政编码：242576）。联系电话：18163656。电子邮箱：xalyg@hxblnksa.biz.cn

Zhù zhǐ: Zhōng Shí Quán Guǎngxī Zhuàngzú Zìzhìqū Guìlín Shì Yángshuò Xiàn Jùn Jiǔ Lù 762 Hào Yuān Tǔ Jiǔ Diàn (Yóuzhèng Biānmǎ：242576). Liánxì Diànhuà：18163656. Diànzǐ Yóuxiāng：xalyg@hxblnksa.biz.cn

Shi Quan Zhong, Yuan Tu Hotel, 762 Jun Jiu Road, Yangshuo County, Guilin, Guangxi Autonomous Region. Postal Code: 242576. Phone Number：18163656. E-mail：xalyg@hxblnksa.biz.cn

1041。姓名: 田福沛

住址（机场）：广西壮族自治区防城港市东兴市己宽路 994 号防城港秀乙国际机场（邮政编码：796821）。联系电话：73982555。电子邮箱：dhxsj@kraiofvx.airports.cn

Zhù zhǐ: Tián Fú Bèi Guǎngxī Zhuàngzú Zìzhìqū Fángchénggǎng Shì Dōng Xīng Shì Jǐ Kuān Lù 994 Hào Fángcénggǎng Xiù Yǐ Guó Jì Jī Chǎng (Yóuzhèng Biānmǎ：796821). Liánxì Diànhuà：73982555. Diànzǐ Yóuxiāng：dhxsj@kraiofvx.airports.cn

Fu Bei Tian, Fangchenggang Xiu Yi International Airport, 994 Ji Kuan Road, Dongxing City, Fangchenggang, Guangxi Autonomous Region. Postal Code: 796821. Phone Number：73982555. E-mail：dhxsj@kraiofvx.airports.cn

1042。姓名: 蒙龙山

住址（博物院）：广西壮族自治区南宁市隆安县郁王路 965 号南宁博物馆（邮政编码：760116）。联系电话：88661153。电子邮箱：clpjs@khfjywuz.museums.cn

Zhù zhǐ: Méng Lóng Shān Guǎngxī Zhuàngzú Zìzhìqū Nánníng Shì Lóngānxiàn Yù Wàng Lù 965 Hào Nánníng Bó Wù Guǎn (Yóuzhèng Biānmǎ：760116). Liánxì Diànhuà：88661153. Diànzǐ Yóuxiāng：clpjs@khfjywuz.museums.cn

Long Shan Meng, NanNing Museum, 965 Yu Wang Road, Longan County, NanNing, Guangxi Autonomous Region. Postal Code: 760116. Phone Number：88661153. E-mail：clpjs@khfjywuz.museums.cn

1043。姓名: 石桥院

住址（大学）：广西壮族自治区柳州市柳江区葆世大学来郁路 547 号（邮政编码：666374）。联系电话：70220007。电子邮箱：qpkej@ipgjuesb.edu.cn

Zhù zhǐ: Shí Qiáo Yuàn Guǎngxī Zhuàngzú Zìzhìqū Liǔzhōu Shì Liǔjiāng Qū Bǎo Shì DàxuéLái Yù Lù 547 Hào (Yóuzhèng Biānmǎ：666374). Liánxì Diànhuà：70220007. Diànzǐ Yóuxiāng：qpkej@ipgjuesb.edu.cn

Qiao Yuan Shi, Bao Shi University, 547 Lai Yu Road, Liujiang District, Liuzhou, Guangxi Autonomous Region. Postal Code: 666374. Phone Number：70220007. E-mail：qpkej@ipgjuesb.edu.cn

1044。姓名: 况洵独

住址（广场）：广西壮族自治区钦州市浦北县咚石路 765 号院己广场（邮政编码：230334）。联系电话：58581749。电子邮箱：tbqyu@gozkcdqn.squares.cn

Zhù zhǐ: Kuàng Xún Dú Guǎngxī Zhuàngzú Zìzhìqū Qīnzhōu Shì Pǔ Běi Xiàn Dōng Shí Lù 765 Hào Yuàn Jǐ Guǎng Chǎng (Yóuzhèng Biānmǎ：230334). Liánxì Diànhuà：58581749. Diànzǐ Yóuxiāng：tbqyu@gozkcdqn.squares.cn

Xun Du Kuang, Yuan Ji Square, 765 Dong Shi Road, Pubei County, Qinzhou, Guangxi Autonomous Region. Postal Code: 230334. Phone Number：58581749. E-mail：tbqyu@gozkcdqn.squares.cn

1045。姓名: 瞿近黎

住址（火车站）：广西壮族自治区钦州市钦南区阳宝路 997 号钦州站（邮政编码：797144）。联系电话：60510107。电子邮箱：ehatl@rwjacehf.chr.cn

Zhù zhǐ: Qú Jìn Lí Guǎngxī Zhuàngzú Zìzhìqū Qīnzhōu Shì Qīn Nán Qū Yáng Bǎo Lù 997 Hào Qīnzōu Zhàn（Yóuzhèng Biānmǎ：797144). Liánxì Diànhuà：60510107. Diànzǐ Yóuxiāng：ehatl@rwjacehf.chr.cn

Jin Li Qu, Qinzhou Railway Station, 997 Yang Bao Road, Chennan District, Qinzhou, Guangxi Autonomous Region. Postal Code: 797144. Phone Number：60510107. E-mail：ehatl@rwjacehf.chr.cn

1046。姓名: 寿坡冕

住址（公共汽车站）：广西壮族自治区贵港市港南区立食路 297 号寰铁站（邮政编码：862139）。联系电话：72784039。电子邮箱：zqdnt@bvnmwygk.transport.cn

Zhù zhǐ: Shòu Pō Miǎn Guǎngxī Zhuàngzú Zìzhìqū Guìgǎng Shì Gǎngnán Qū Lì Shí Lù 297 Hào Huán Tiě Zhàn（Yóuzhèng Biānmǎ：862139). Liánxì Diànhuà：72784039. Diànzǐ Yóuxiāng：zqdnt@bvnmwygk.transport.cn

Po Mian Shou, Huan Tie Bus Station, 297 Li Shi Road, Konan District, Guigang, Guangxi Autonomous Region. Postal Code: 862139. Phone Number：72784039. E-mail：zqdnt@bvnmwygk.transport.cn

1047。姓名: 怀计岐

住址（湖泊）：广西壮族自治区百色市靖西市龙泽路 803 号彬近湖（邮政编码：906827）。联系电话：53014660。电子邮箱：gnhvd@cqgdkxmz.lakes.cn

Zhù zhǐ: Huái Jì Qí Guǎngxī Zhuàngzú Zìzhìqū Bǎisè Shì Jìng Xī Shì Lóng Zé Lù 803 Hào Bīn Jìn Hú（Yóuzhèng Biānmǎ：906827). Liánxì Diànhuà：53014660. Diànzǐ Yóuxiāng：gnhvd@cqgdkxmz.lakes.cn

Ji Qi Huai, Bin Jin Lake, 803 Long Ze Road, Jingxi, Baise, Guangxi Autonomous Region. Postal Code: 906827. Phone Number：53014660. E-mail：gnhvd@cqgdkxmz.lakes.cn

1048。姓名: 羊舌寰译

住址（寺庙）：广西壮族自治区河池市东兰县友福路 423 号阳科寺（邮政编码：529642）。联系电话：25587917。电子邮箱：xqnul@eopiwvra.god.cn

Zhù zhǐ: Yángshé Huán Yì Guǎngxī Zhuàngzú Zìzhìqū Héchí Shì Dōng Lán Xiàn Yǒu Fú Lù 423 Hào Yáng Kē Sì（Yóuzhèng Biānmǎ：529642). Liánxì Diànhuà：25587917. Diànzǐ Yóuxiāng：xqnul@eopiwvra.god.cn

Huan Yi Yangshe, Yang Ke Temple, 423 You Fu Road, Donglan County, Hechi, Guangxi Autonomous Region. Postal Code: 529642. Phone Number：25587917. E-mail：xqnul@eopiwvra.god.cn

1049。姓名: 薛熔进

住址（医院）：广西壮族自治区玉林市博白县黎智路 265 号成铁医院（邮政编码：807007）。联系电话：34743709。电子邮箱：ambgj@bkrtjpin.health.cn

Zhù zhǐ: Xuē Róng Jìn Guǎngxī Zhuàngzú Zìzhìqū Yùlín Shì Bó Bái Xiàn Lí Zhì Lù 265 Hào Chéng Tiě Yī Yuàn（Yóuzhèng Biānmǎ：807007). Liánxì Diànhuà：34743709. Diànzǐ Yóuxiāng：ambgj@bkrtjpin.health.cn

Rong Jin Xue, Cheng Tie Hospital, 265 Li Zhi Road, Bobai County, Yulin, Guangxi Autonomous Region. Postal Code: 807007. Phone Number：34743709. E-mail：ambgj@bkrtjpin.health.cn

1050。姓名: 杜领中

住址（博物院）：广西壮族自治区梧州市藤县铁院路 361 号梧州博物馆（邮政编码：688020）。联系电话：67245713。电子邮箱：
tixmd@rsjoqzvb.museums.cn

Zhù zhǐ: Dù Lǐng Zhòng Guǎngxī Zhuàngzú Zìzhìqū Wúzhōu Shì Téng Xiàn Fū Yuàn Lù 361 Hào Wúzōu Bó Wù Guǎn (Yóuzhèng Biānmǎ：688020). Liánxì Diànhuà：67245713. Diànzǐ Yóuxiāng：tixmd@rsjoqzvb.museums.cn

Ling Zhong Du, Wuzhou Museum, 361 Fu Yuan Road, Fuji County, Wuzhou, Guangxi Autonomous Region. Postal Code: 688020. Phone Number：67245713. E-mail：tixmd@rsjoqzvb.museums.cn